JUSTICE, EQUAL OPPORTUNITY, AND THE FAMILY

JAMES S. FISHKIN

YALE UNIVERSITY PRESS
NEW HAVEN AND LONDON

Published with assistance from the foundation
established in memory of Philip Hamilton McMillan
of the Class of 1894, Yale College.

Designed by Sally Harris
and set in Trump Medieval type by
Coghill Composition Company.
Printed in the United States of America by
Halliday Lithograph, West Hanover, Mass.

Library of Congress Cataloging in Publication Data

Fishkin, James S.
  Justice, equal opportunity, and the family.

  Includes bibliographical references and index.
  1. Equality.   2. Justice.   3. Family.
4. Liberalism.   I. Title.
JC578.F57   1983   320'.01'1   82 – 10939
ISBN 0 – 300 – 02865 – 2
ISBN 0 – 300 – 03249 – 8

10   9   8   7   6   5   4   3   2

CONTENTS

Acknowledgments   vii
1. INTRODUCTION   1
2. EQUAL OPPORTUNITY AND THE FAMILY   11
    2.1   Distributive Justice: Three Problems   11
    2.2   The Principle of Merit   19
    2.3   Equality of Life Chances   30
    2.4   The Autonomy of the Family   35

3. THE TRILEMMA OF EQUAL OPPORTUNITY   44
    3.1   Ideal Theory   44
    3.2   Background Inequalities   47
    3.3   The First Option   51
    3.4   The Second Option   55
    3.5   The Third Option   64
    3.6   Strategies of Intervention   67
    3.7   Preferential Treatment and Compensation for the Past   82

4. FAIRNESS, GROUP COMPENSATION, AND EQUALITY: RESPONSES TO THE TRILEMMA   106
    4.1   Fairness and Merit   107
    4.2   Competition and Lotteries   110
    4.3   Group Competition and Compensation   113
    4.4   Unequal Positions   131
    4.5   Policy Implications   146

5. OPTIONS FOR LIBERAL THEORY   152
    5.1   Contemporary Liberalism: The General Issue   152
    5.2   Living with Inconclusiveness   169

Index   195

ACKNOWLEDGMENTS

My work on this book was generously supported by a research grant from the National Endowment for the Humanities. The manuscript was completed during a fellowship at the Woodrow Wilson International Center for Scholars in Washington, D.C., in the spring and summer of 1981. This support is gratefully acknowledged. Several colleagues and friends gave me crucial help at various stages. I would especially like to thank Bruce Ackerman, Brian Barry, Robert Dahl, Richard Flathman, William Galston, Douglas Rae, and Bernard Williams. I would also like to thank Richard R. Nelson and Charles E. Lindblom, present and past directors of Yale's Institution for Social and Policy Studies. They have created an environment in which conversations connecting political theory and public policy flourish spontaneously and this book is one result.

1. INTRODUCTION

Equal opportunity is the central doctrine in modern liberalism for legitimating the distribution of goods in society. Rather than being concerned with equality of outcomes, liberalism, in both theory and practice, has been concerned with the rationing of opportunities for people to become unequal. Inequality has found a justification in the basic idea of a fair competition among individuals for unequal positions in society. This idea, sometimes dismissed as weakly reformist or even conservative, is, in fact, startlingly radical in its implications. If taken seriously, it would require systematic intrusions into the family and a vast reform in the way of life we commonly take for granted.

The family is the one crucial source of inequality in modern society that has gone largely unexamined in the theory of distributive justice. Inequalities between the races, between the sexes, between states, between generations, inequalities that result from market forces, from genetic differences, from the political process—all of these inequalities have become familiar issues in recent moral and political theory.[1] But the

1. Each of these issues has produced a vast literature. Representative examples include Marshall Cohen, Thomas Nagel, and Thomas Scanlon, eds., *Equality and Preferential Treatment* (Princeton: Princeton University Press, 1977) on racial and sexual equality; Charles R. Beitz, *Political Theory and International Relations* (Princeton: Princeton University Press, 1974) and Michael Walzer, *Just and Unjust Wars* (New York: Basic Books, 1977) on justice between states; R. I. Sikora and Brian Barry, eds., *Obligations to Future Generations* (Philadelphia: Temple University Press, 1978) on justice between generations; Charles E. Lindblom, *Politics and Markets* (New York: Basic

1

role of the family in generating inequalities—while the subject of extensive empirical study[2]—has not been systematically incorporated into normative debate. No defensible and coherent ideal of distribution can afford so serious an omission.

Perhaps the family has been largely invisible in liberal theory because of the latter's individualistic presuppositions. Liberalism presents us with a picture of isolated, atomic individuals who seem to spring from nowhere in order to experience utility or claim rights or enjoy liberties and then vanish. My argument is that any systematic attempt to apply common liberal assumptions to the normal process by which these individuals are created and nurtured must break down. A pattern of new and difficult choices emerges. This pattern will require that we modify our commitment to one or another in a series of crucial liberal assumptions, all of which had previously seemed fully realizable.

In many ways, this argument is a new variation on an old theme: the conflicts between liberty and equality. Both principles have maintained an important place in the liberal tradition—a tradition that can, in fact, be viewed as a continuing dialogue about the relative place of the two principles.[3]

Books, 1977) on the impact of market forces; N. J. Block and Gerald Dworkin, eds., *The IQ Controversy* (New York: Pantheon, 1976) on genetic differences; and James S. Fishkin, ed., *Symposium on the Theory and Practice of Representation*, a special issue of *Ethics* 91, no. 3 (April 1981), on political equality.

2. See, for example, James S. Coleman et al., *Equality of Educational Opportunity*, 2 vols., U.S., Dept. of Health, Education, and Welfare, Office of Education, (Washington, D.C.: Government Printing Office, 1966); Christopher Jencks et al., *Inequality* (New York: Basic Books, 1972) and Christopher Jencks et al., *Who Gets Ahead? The Determinants of Economic Success in America* (New York: Basic Books, 1979); Frederick Mosteller and Daniel P. Moynihan, eds., *On Equality of Educational Opportunity* (New York: Vintage Books, 1972); Richard H. DeLone, *Small Futures: Children, Inequality, and the Limits of Liberal Reform* (New York: Harcourt Brace Jovanovich, 1977); and Samuel Bowles and Herbert Gintis, *Schooling in Capitalist America* (New York: Basic Books, 1976).

3. Two recent interpretations of the liberal tradition in terms of the tension between liberty and equality can be found in J. Roland Pennock, *Democratic Theory* (Princeton: Princeton University Press, 1979) and Amy Gutmann, *Liberal Equality* (Cambridge: Cambridge University Press, 1980).

Libertarians have formulated this conflict most dramatically. The interferences with liberty that would be required in order to maintain equality of outcomes have been a recurring nightmare for them.[4] Liberals, on the other hand, have usually managed to defuse the problem by aspiring to realize only a less demanding form of equality. Instead of equality of outcomes, they have focused on equality of opportunities. By prescribing only some appropriate equalization of opportunities to become unequal, liberals have managed to fend off the charge that their egalitarian aspirations would require continuous government interference with liberty in order to maintain, over time, a particular distributional structure (such as equality of outcomes).[5]

I will argue, however, that this apparent success in avoiding conflicts with liberty is only illusory. If taken seriously, the liberal strategy of attempting to ration fairly opportunities for the achievement of unequal positions would require systematic intrusions into the family. Only then could the maintenance of background inequalities be rendered compatible with equal opportunities for the development of talents and other

4. See, for example, F. A. Hayek, *Law, Legislation and Liberty, Vol. 2, The Mirage of Social Justice* (London, Routledge and Kegan Paul, 1976); and Robert Nozick, *Anarchy, State, and Utopia* (New York: Basic Books, 1974) especially part 2. I will return to this issue in section 4.4 below.

5. Two particularly important attempts in recent liberal theory to prescribe equal opportunities for the achievement of unequal positions can be found in John Rawls, *A Theory of Justice* (Cambridge: Harvard University Press, 1971), particularly chapter 2 and Bruce Ackerman, *Social Justice in the Liberal State* (New Haven: Yale University Press, 1980), particularly part 2. Two important works probing the limits of this strategy are Bernard Williams's "The Idea of Equality" in Peter Laslett and W. G. Runciman, eds., *Philosophy, Politics and Society, Second Series* (Oxford: Basil Blackwell, 1962), pp. 110–31 and Douglas Rae et al., *Equalities* (Cambridge: Harvard University Press, 1981), particularly chapter 4. For claims about the central role of equal opportunity in the American political tradition see J. R. Pole, *The Pursuit of Equality in American History* (Berkeley: University of California Press, 1978); and David M. Potter, *People of Plenty* (Chicago: University of Chicago Press, 1954), particularly chapter 5. For a critical discussion of the legitimating function for inequalities served by meritocratic notions of equal opportunity see Bowles and Gintis, *Schooling*, part 2.

qualifications. The conflict with liberty, in other words, cannot be avoided. Rather, it reappears in a particularly excruciating form, directed at the family.

Once the role of the family is taken into account, the apparently moderate aspiration of equal opportunity produces conflicts with the private sphere of liberty—with autonomous family relations—that are nothing short of intractable. Elements that are essential to the liberal doctrine of equal opportunity come into irreconcilable conflict with the private core of the notion of liberty, the portion that touches most of our lives most directly.

These conflicts can be formulated in terms of three assumptions—two central liberal assumptions about equal opportunity, on the one hand, and our common moral assumptions about the family, on the other. The first liberal assumption might be called the *principle of merit.* According to this assumption, there should be widespread procedural fairness in the evaluation of qualifications for positions. No discrimination should be permitted on the basis of race, sex, class, ethnic origin, or other irrelevant characteristics. While there are many interesting controversies about how qualifications for positions ought to be defined, the principle of merit in some form is a basic and familiar element in the liberal credo.[6]

The second assumption might be called equality of life chances. According to this notion, I should not be able to enter a hospital ward of healthy newborn babies and, on the basis of class, race, sex, or other arbitrary native characteristics, predict the eventual positions in society of those children. Of course, there are many different ways of evaluating their eventual positions. By whatever plausible criterion these evaluations are made, however, it should be clear that in this society, I can confidently make such predictions.[7]

---

6. For a detailed discussion of merit see section 2.2 below.
7. See, for example, Jencks, *Who Gets Ahead?* pp. 81-83 and DeLone, *Small Futures,* pp. 3–19. The independent cumulative effects of meritocratic sorting

These two assumptions can both be defended in terms of the basic liberal approach to equal opportunity, namely, the notion that there should be fair competition among individuals for unequal positions in society. Henceforth, I will refer to this basic notion as the *fair competition* assumption. The two principles just defined can be viewed as explications, respectively, of what might be meant by "competition" in this context and of what might be meant, in any ultimately defensible sense, by "fairness."[8] On the one hand, the principle of merit is merely the claim that the competition should be in terms of qualifications relevant to job performance in the positions to be filled. The principle of equal life chances, on the other hand, can be viewed as the central condition that would render the competition fair. If one can predict where people will end up in the competition merely by knowing their race or sex or family background, then the conditions under which their talents and motivations have developed must be grossly unequal. It is unfair that some persons are given every conceivable advantage while others never really have a chance, in the first place, to develop their talents. The principle of equal life chances, when combined with the principle of merit, would require equal developmental conditions for talent development.

When these two assumptions about equal opportunity are combined with a third assumption, the *autonomy of the family*—permitting parents to substantially influence the development of their children—a pattern of difficult choices emerges. This pattern takes the form of a "trilemma," a kind of dilemma with three corners. I will argue that commitment to any two of these assumptions rules out the third. Attempting to maintain all three assumptions—the principle of merit, equality of life

on the distribution of life chances are investigated by Raymond Boudon in *Education, Opportunity and Social Inequality* (New York: John Wiley & Sons, Inc., 1974).

8. There are, of course, some notions of procedural fairness in the very notion of a competition. But without equality of life chances, the competition lacks background fairness. See section 2.3 below.

chances, and the autonomy of the family—would be like attempting to hold up a three-cornered stool when only two legs are available. No matter which two corners one chooses to hold up, lack of the third is enough to undermine the whole structure.

I will defend this claim for ideal theory. It would be less surprising if one or more of our central assumptions had to be sacrificed under unfavorable conditions where extreme scarcity, lack of compliance, or a historical legacy of injustice made any particular principle difficult to implement.[9] My argument, rather, is that under the best conditions that might realistically be imagined for a large-scale industrial society, this trilemma arises. In this sense, the basic liberal approach to equal opportunity does not amount to a coherent ideal once complications involving the family are systematically taken into account.

Thus far, the argument may be considered a kind of thought experiment testing the viability of the basic liberal approach to equal opportunity—the assignment of persons to unequal positions according to a fair competition—when that approach is combined with our common assumptions about the autonomy of the family. Either systematic intrusions into the family would be required to equalize developmental conditions despite unequal outcomes or the whole liberal focus on equal opportunities—as distinct from equal outcomes—would have to be abandoned.

This difficulty with equal opportunity can also be viewed as part of a more general problem confronting liberal theory. It has been characteristic of liberalism, in both theory and practice, to accept background inequalities provided that certain process-related equalities are maintained.[10] Assignment to positions in a fair system of equal opportunity is only one such process equality. Political equality, or equal consideration of one's preferences by the political system, is another. Equality

9. See section 3.1 below for a discussion of ideal theory.
10. See section 5.1 below for further discussion of these process equalities.

before the law, or equal consideration of one's claims by the judicial system, is a third central process equality. A fourth, which has had serious advocates, is equal consideration of one's health care needs by the medical care system. In each of these cases the central liberal aspiration has been to institutionalize practices that would grant everyone's claims equal consideration—whether in the political sphere, or before the judicial system or the medical care system, or as in the case of equal opportunity, in the system of job assignment. In each of these cases, the attempt to institutionalize equal consideration in a selected sphere of life (for example, politics, the courts, or the system of job assignment) cannot be realized while *both* background inequalities and certain key liberties are maintained. As we shall see, the background inequalities spill over onto the process, undermining its claim to equality. And attempts either to insulate the process or to eliminate the inequalities directly, would exact, in turn, a substantial cost in liberty.

Hence, I will argue that the trilemma of equal opportunity to be explored at length here offers a theoretical case study of a more general difficulty facing liberal theory. No commonly recognizable version of liberalism today could do without a doctrine of equal opportunity any more than it could do without a doctrine of political equality or of equality before the law. Yet I will argue that these familiar process equalities are all subject to a general version of the trilemma. In each case, without systematic attempts at insulation, background inequalities, both social and economic, undermine the claim to equal consideration in any meaningful sense. It is not only true that those from the higher strata have greater life chances and more than equal opportunities; they also have greater than equal influence on the political process and greater than equal consideration from the health care and legal systems. In each of these cases, something closer to full equality in the process could be systematically restored—but at a cost in liberty. Just as the liberty of families to influence the development of their children would have to be restricted to fully realize equal opportunity, other liberties would have to be restricted for each of the other process equalities. For example, the Supreme Court ruled in the controversial case of *Buckley* v. *Valeo* that the First Amendment protects expenditures advocating the election or defeat of political candidates. Such expenditures could only be restricted, the court reasoned, at a cost to liberty of expression and association.[11] Yet such restrictions would be required for any systematic barrier preventing unequal economic resources from being translated into unequal political influence. Similarly, the liberty of individuals to choose, and pay for, their own lawyers, doctors, and related services would be at stake in any effort to fully equalize consideration by the judicial and health care systems of the claims of individuals, regardless of class or income throughout the society.

In each of these cases, the strategy of insulating background inequalities from the process in question could only come at some cost in liberty. Failing to insulate, however, would seriously undermine the claim to equality, for it would be to accept that the less advantaged have less than equal opportunities, or less than equal political influence, or less than equal consideration of their claims or interests from the legal or medical care systems. To accept such implications under ideal theory, under the best conditions that might realistically be imagined for modern industrial societies, would be to admit that liberalism can only offer a seriously tarnished and compromised ideal for public policy.[12]

I will thus argue that the stark conflicts involving equal opportunity to be explored here represent a particularly disturbing version of a more general difficulty. In broad outlines,

---

11. Buckley v. Valeo, 424 U.S. 1 (1976). See also First National Bank v. Bellotti, 435 U.S. 765 (1978). For a general discussion of the issues raised by these cases see David Adamany, "PAC's and the Democratic Financing of Politics," *Arizona Law Review* 22, no. 2 (1980): 569–602. See also the discussion below in section 5.1.

12. See sections 5.1 and 5.2 below.

it is that those process equalities that are at the core of modern liberalism can be maintained only at a substantial cost in liberty. This is unavoidable because the process equalities can be maintained only if either (i) they are systematically insulated from background inequalities, or (ii) those background inequalities are, themselves, eliminated. Either strategy, insulation or elimination, would require a substantial cost in liberty. Systematic conflicts between liberty and these merely process-related equalities are thus unavoidable. Defensible versions of liberal theory cannot casually affirm fundamentally incompatible commitments and, at the same time, aspire to offer us a unified and coherent ideal for public policy.

It might be argued that in the pages that follow I am taking certain principles too seriously. I make an issue, too quickly, out of the fact that they cannot be *fully* realized in a manner compatible with other key principles. I would reply, however, that the argument takes place under the conditions of *ideal theory*, that is, under the most favorable conditions that can be realistically imagined for a modern industrial society. We learn something central about the character of our most fundamental principles if they stand in irreconcilable conflict under such conditions. We learn that they do not define a *unified and coherent ideal* that we can aspire to implement. Rather, they add up only to a collection of conflicting considerations, each one of which would take public policy in a quite different direction if it were given further emphasis.

Perhaps no general solution at the level of first principles needs to be found for this pattern of hard choices. A less ambitious form of liberal theory, one committed only to root conflicting principles to be traded-off in particular cases, will be sketched at the end. While less satisfying than some new and exceptionless first principle, it may be a more honest response to the true difficulties of the trilemmas to be explored here. In broad outline, this book will move from the specific issue of equal opportunity, to the general version of the trilemma applied to other process equalities, and to certain recurring sources of inconclusiveness in theories that aspire to offer any more systematic solution.

In the end, I will argue that if we can learn to expect less, we may find a great deal to be satisfied with in a limited liberalism, one that frankly accepts these recurring conflicts, even under ideal conditions. Instead of offering a single coherent vision of the just society, to be gradually approached, such a limited liberalism will focus on identifying the complex variety of factors to be weighed against each other in particular cases. It would consist of *ideals without an ideal,* of conflicting principles without a unified vision in clear focus. Whether others can arrive at defensible versions that are more systematic will depend, I believe, on how they face up to the hard choices to be explored below.

2. EQUAL OPPORTUNITY
AND THE FAMILY

2.1 Distributive Justice:
Three Problems

Distributive justice may be thought of as a conjunction of three problems: (a) the problem of value, (b) the problem of structure, and (c) the problem of assignment. The first is the issue of *what* should be considered in questions of distribution (for example, utility, income, status, primary goods); the second is the issue of *how* it ought to be distributed (for example, to increase equality, to raise the minimum, or to raise the total); the third is the issue of *to whom* it ought to be distributed (that is, how opportunities for valuable positions ought to be rationed).

My focus in this book will be on the problem of assignment. My claim will be that even if the extremely controversial issues arising from any known proposals directed at the first two problems were resolved, the third problem, of assignment, would be intractable within the framework of common liberal assumptions—once the role of the family were systematically taken into account.

There are well-known difficulties applying to the first two problems. While I will not focus on them here, they are worth identifying briefly in order to place our discussion in context. By the problem of value, I mean the issue of what it is that is valuable to individuals whose distribution is being assessed. Is it income and wealth? Is it utility? Does it include rights and liberties (as in the case of John Rawls's theory of "primary goods")?[1] Theories of value defined in terms of the satisfaction

1. John Rawls, *Theory of Justice*, especially pp. 90–95 and 395–99. For a general discussion of solutions to the problem of value see my *Tyranny and*

11

of actual wants or preferences must face the well-known conundrums arising from efforts to make interpersonal comparisons of subjective satisfaction.[2] On the other hand, theories of value not defined in terms of such actual wants or preferences face an alternative challenge—justifying paternalistic inferences, in other words, claims that a person is better or worse off although his *own* wants and preferences would support a conflicting assessment.[3]

If we somehow surmounted these difficulties with a workable theory of value, a workable theory of *what* was being assessed for distribution, we would arrive immediately at a second basic issue: what is the best structure of distribution for that value? Should more equal distributions be preferred? Or distributions with a higher total? Or perhaps those with a higher minimum?

Each of the principles just mentioned is purely *structural;* given any two situations one can determine which is better (or rank them as equally good) based entirely on the information available from a listing of payoffs to positions. By payoffs I mean shares of value as specified by some answer to the first problem discussed above. By positions I mean either individuals listed in the order of their shares of value or numerically equal groupings of individuals (n-tiles, each consisting of $1/n$ of the population) listed in order of their shares of value.

Purely structural principles require no information apart

Legitimacy: A Critique of Political Theories (Baltimore: Johns Hopkins, 1979), chapter 3.

2. See Lionel Robbins's famous article "Interpersonal Comparisons of Utility: A Comment," *Economic Journal* 48, no. 192 (1938): 635–41 and I. M. D. Little, *A Critique of Welfare Economics* 2nd ed. (Oxford: Oxford University Press, 1957). For an assertion that at least some rough interpersonal comparisons of intensity are possible, see Little, p. 53 and A. K. Sen, *Collective Choice and Social Welfare* (San Francisco: Holden Day, 1970) pp. 79–102.

3. Rawlsian primary goods offer an example. For a critique of Rawls's account of primary goods see my "Justice and Rationality: Some Objections to the Central Argument in Rawls's Theory" *American Political Science Review* 69, no. 2 (June 1979): 615–29. For a general claim about the paternalistic burden facing such theories, see my *Tyranny and Legitimacy,* chapter 3.

from such a listing. We can determine, for example, which situation is more equal, which has a higher total, or which has a higher minimum merely by reference to this kind of listing. Elsewhere, I have argued that such purely structural principles must be, by themselves, inadequate as ethical criteria for social choice. As we will see in a moment, they take no account of assignment—how persons may or may not be moved around from one position to another in the structure. Through this insensitivity to assignment, structural principles may legitimate severe deprivations that are entirely avoidable.[4]

Of course, some theorists (most notably Nozick) have denied any role whatsoever for structural considerations. But such theorists are committed, as a result, to legitimating some outcomes regardless of structural considerations, regardless of how minimal the bottom share becomes, or how unequal the disparity in shares is, or how much the aggregate public welfare declines.[5] Most theorists would not accept such implications.

The structural considerations just referred to—equality, aggregate utility, and Rawlsian maximin justice (requiring maximization of the minimum share)[6] are the structural principles most prominent in contemporary theory. Each of them, however, is vulnerable to obvious objections.

Equality, as Rawls points out forcefully, can make everyone worse-off, including those at the bottom. Consider this simplified choice (where the numbers represent some index of primary goods or utilities to each representative position in society under situations A and B, respectively).

4. This argument is developed at length in *Tyranny and Legitimacy,* chapter 10. See the examples in section 2.3 below.

5. Robert Nozick, *Anarchy, State, and Utopia.* For further criticisms of Nozick along these lines see, H. L. A. Hart, "Between Utility and Rights," in *The Idea of Freedom: Essays in Honor of Isaiah Berlin,* ed. Alan Ryan (Oxford: Oxford University Press, 1979) pp. 77–98 and my *Tyranny and Legitimacy,* chapter 9.

6. By Rawlsian maximin justice I mean his general conception that requires equal distributions unless unequal distributions of primary goods will be to the advantage of the least fortunate. (See Rawls, *Theory of Justice,* p. 303.)

Situation A	Situation B
3	4
3	6
3	8
3	9

Everyone, including the person who is worst-off, is better off in situation B. The leveling approach to equality can be ruinous to all.

Utilitarianism, on the other hand, captures the interests of all—but in a manner entirely insensitive to differing distributions of the same aggregate quantity of utility. To take two simplified alternatives, consider the choice between situations A and B below.

Situation A	Situation B
100	0
100	0
100	0
100	400

There is no moral question, for a utilitarian, in the choice between A and B. They must be ranked precisely equal because they have precisely the same aggregate utility (and, of course, the same average utility since population is constant). B must be *as good* as A even though B involves severe sacrifices for three out of four persons while everyone is well-off under A. And, of course, if the total under B were 401 (instead of 400), then a utilitarian would be required to prefer B to A.

The utilitarian insensitivity to the special moral claim of the lowest stratum is remedied by maximin. Rawls's general conception of justice (that the minimum share of primary goods should be maximized) is the remaining structural solution which has been particularly prominent in recent discussions. But how special is the moral claim of the lowest stratum? Maximin is entirely insensitive to all harms and benefits to strata other than the minimum. Rawls himself questions whether the justice or injustice of billions of dollars to higher strata should turn on whether the lowest stratum is improved by a penny or so.[7] He hypothesizes that these possibilities are unlikely to arise. Yet there is no adequate empirical basis for ruling out such possibilities. If the "bucket" by which we redistribute to the minimum is sufficiently "leaky,"[8] we may be faced with choices like the following:

Situation A	Situation B
3.99999	4
15	4
20	4
50	4

Maximin will place any improvement, however slight for the bottom stratum, above all interests, however great, of all other strata.

These difficulties are instances of a more general dilemma. The principles we commonly apply to the problem of structure fall into two categories. One kind of principle is aggregative—it is indifferent between all possible distributions of the same aggregate quantity of goods or welfare. Classical and average utilitarianism are preeminent examples. A second major category consists in principles that are distributive. A distributive principle prescribes a state of affairs if, and only if, it improves the (relative or absolute) standing of (one or more of) the less fortunate strata.[9] Hence maximin is a distributive principle

7. See Rawls, page 157: "Yet it seems extraordinary that the justice of increasing the expectations of the better placed by a billion dollars, say, should turn on whether the prospects of the least favored increase or decrease by a penny." His reply on the next page: "The possibilities which the objection envisages cannot arise in real cases; the feasible set is so restricted that they are excluded."

8. For the "leaky bucket" analogy, see Arthur M. Okun, *Equality and Efficiency: The Big Trade-Off* (Washington, D.C.: The Brookings Institution, 1975), pp. 90–120.

9. I borrow this terminology from an illuminating discussion in Brian Barry, *Political Argument* (London: Routledge and Kegan Paul, 1965), p. 43. I have

because it prescribes choices based entirely on whether they improve the standing of the bottom stratum. Equality, similarly, is a distributive principle because it prescribes situations based entirely on whether they improve the relative standing of less fortunate strata (which might be defined as those below the median).

The dilemma facing any solution to the problem of structure is that any aggregative principle (such as utilitarianism) is necessarily insensitive to distributive objections that must, at some point, if they are great enough, become overwhelming; and any distributive principle (such as maximin or equality) is necessarily insensitive to aggregative objections that must also, at some point, if they are great enough, become decisive. While there have been some efforts to develop hybrid principles incorporating features from both aggregative and distributive principles, adequate versions of such approaches remain to be developed.[10] Hence the problem of structure has proved no more susceptible to easy solution than has the problem of value.

My focus here, however, will be on the third basic issue in theories of distributive justice, the problem of *assignment: who gets what position in the structure?*

As noted above, many familiar principles are formulated so that they do not have to take account of this issue at all. Consider the three columns below:

---

modified the definitions, however, in order to employ them here. Barry defines distributive principles more generally to include any criteria that prescribe how a given quantity is to be distributed. My more restrictive definition is meant to limit it to those principles which are especially compelling in their conflict with aggregative considerations. A distributive principle in Barry's broader sense might, for example, require that all increases be given to the top stratum. Such a principle would not play a role in the fundamental dilemma outlined here.

10. For one particularly bold effort, see Douglas Rae, "A Principle of Simple Justice," in Peter Laslett and James Fishkin, eds., *Philosophy, Politics and Society, Fifth Series* (New Haven: Yale University Press, 1979), pp. 134–54. As Rae was the first to point out, his hybrid principle—by permitting the alternation of independent aggregative and distributive clauses—violates transitivity.

Positions	Payoffs	Persons
P_1	S_1	I_1
P_2	S_2	I_2
P_3	S_3	I_3
P_4	S_4	I_4
P_5	S_5	I_5

By positions I mean groupings of persons according to their payoffs or shares of whatever value (income, primary goods, utility) is under discussion. So in this case, those in the top fifth, position P_1, receive payoffs of S_1, those in the second fifth, P_2, receive payoffs of S_2, and so on. Of course, positions may be divided however finely one might wish into n-tiles and one may, thus, specify the payoffs for each 1/n of the population. Utilitarianism, equality, and maximin (the maximize the minimum share principle) are all examples of purely structural criteria in that they need reference only to these two columns, positions and payoffs, to evaluate a situation or compare it to another. From a mere listing of payoffs to positions, in other words, one can determine the aggregate or average utility, the extent of equality, or the size of the minimum share. From this information alone, there is no way of knowing how *persons* are assigned to positions. The information offered us by the first two columns abstracts from the life history of individuals over time. It does not tell us how persons acquire and maintain positions in the structure.

Consider, for example, two alternative societies that are structurally identical. By this I mean that the payoffs to positions as specified by our first two columns are exactly the same. One of these societies offers equal and widespread opportunities to all strata, ethnic groups, and races in the society. The other society, however, practices systematic apartheid throughout its system of assignment so that it is divided rigidly on racial grounds into distinct sub-societies within the same geographical territory. Despite such a division, if payoffs to positions are calculated for the entire apartheid society, the statistics when aggregated into a single set of figures are identical to our first society. The overall structure of aggregate welfare, of inequality, and of well-being at the bottom, and so forth, are all identical in the two societies as represented by aggregate statistics. Yet the process of assigning people to positions is starkly different. In the apartheid society racial classifications play a decisive role whereas in our first society they do not. Blacks are differentially assigned to the lower positions (and perhaps some segregated middle positions) while whites are differently assigned to the upper positions (and perhaps some segregated middle positions). By contrast, race plays no role in the assignment process in the other, structurally identical society.

This kind of example reveals, I believe, the inadequacy of any *purely* structural principle of justice. For any purely structural principle, defined so that it can determine choices between any two situations based merely on an account of payoffs to positions, would have to be indifferent between these two societies. Within such a framework, there is no room even for stating the moral issue most of us would raise about the apartheid society compared to its structurally identical alternative.

Or consider a less blatant example. Suppose that in one of the two societies, members of the bottom stratum, I_5 in the column labeled "persons," have no realistic chance of ever aspiring to the higher positions. Over time, if we took a series of structural snapshots of the distribution, groups I_1 through I_4 would change considerably in their assignment according to some process of equal opportunity. Group I_5, however, would always maintain its position at the bottom. And this great inequality in life chances, we might assume, perpetuates itself from one generation to the next. If this system were compared to one that was structurally identical while endowing all strata with roughly equal life chances, most of us, presumably, would see strong reasons for preferring the latter arrangement. Yet this preference cannot be formulated, or defended, within the framework of purely structural principles, that is, the framework provided by answers to only our first two problems above.

The central point is that purely structural principles have no way of accounting for effects on persons that are independent of effects on positions. Yet, it is persons, not ranked positions, who would experience the effects of distributive justice or injustice. It is their life histories that are at stake, and criteria that ignore such effects must be inadequate. They must be supplemented by criteria for assignment to positions—criteria for how persons may, or may not, justifiably be moved around from one position to another.

However the first two problems—value and structure—are resolved, my general point will be that the third one, assignment, poses a special challenge for liberal theory. I have noted some of the distinctive theoretical issues applying to the problems of value and structure. These issues, while open and contested, have generated well-known controversies. Yet the true difficulty of the third issue, assignment, has never been squarely faced because liberal theorists have, for some mystifying reason, been blind to its systematic connections with the family. Hence, while realizing that the first two issues are far from settled, I will focus on certain distinctive claims about the true difficulties of the third—difficulties that would apply even if the first two problems were settled beyond question.

2.2 *The Principle*
of Merit
The issue that I dubbed the problem of assignment in the last section has been formulated within liberal theory as the issue of equal opportunity. In other words, people should be assigned positions according to the basic competitive assumption stated earlier: there should be a fair competition among individuals for unequal positions in society.

It is worth noting that some formal or narrow constructions of equal opportunity would require no more than an impartial assessment of talents and other qualifications relevant to the positions to be filled. I say "no more than" because this requirement is open to powerful objections unless it is supplemented by criteria specifying an appropriate chance to *develop* the desired talents and/or other qualifications in the first place. There is, for this reason, a strong impulsion within liberal theory to undertake a two-fold commitment: a principle of merit (or impartial competition of talents and qualifications, as developed) and a principle of equal life chances specifying roughly equal expectations for everyone regardless of the conditions into which they are born. Obviously, assignment by merit and equal life chances would be simultaneously achieved only when the causal conditions for talent development were substantially equalized across all sectors of society. I will call the demanding position that fully embraces both principles the *strong doctrine of equal opportunity*.

Rawls offers a prime recent example of a liberal theorist who embraces both components of this strong doctrine of equal opportunity. He wishes, however, to maintain this commitment and, at the same time, to maintain the family in much its present form.[11] By contrast, I will argue that if these two component notions of equal opportunity are combined with our customary notions about the family, a trilemma results. Fulfillment of any two of these assumptions can realistically be expected to preclude the third. Liberal theorists must either modify their commitment to one component or the other of the strong doctrine of equal opportunity, or they must accept the radical implications of their position for the family. Unless they face squarely this pattern of conflicting assumptions, they will have failed to offer a systematic and coherent ideal of social justice.[12]

11. See my discussion in section 5.1 below.
12. I am assuming that each of these commitments is a "strong" one. Note that these principles are *not* formulated so as merely to apply ceteris paribus or prima facie. They are formulated without exceptions or qualifications so that any sacrifices in merit, equal life chances, or family autonomy must be considered violations of the stated principle, even in cases where one of these

Let us turn now to the first half of this strong doctrine of equal opportunity. The principle of merit is a common feature of liberal approaches to equal opportunity. Strikingly, it was asserted by both sides in the DeFunis and Bakke controversies over preferential treatment in university admissions.[13] At least in public debate, there has been an "apparent unanimity regarding hiring by competence" (one formulation of this principle).[14] This general kind of principle has achieved wide support, both on grounds of fairness and of efficiency.[15] Even those theorists who explicitly criticize it have usually adopted the strategy exemplified by Rawls—they incorporate it into their own proposal as a necessary *part* of an adequate account of equal opportunity.[16]

principles conflicts with another. Whether we can arrive at one or more principles for this problem that can be defensibly applied without exceptions or qualifications, or whether we should construe these principles as susceptible to an "intuitionistic" process of "trading off" or balancing is an issue we shall return to in section 5.2. The strong and weak terminology is standard. It can be found, for example, in David Lyons, *The Forms and Limits of Utilitarianism* (Oxford: Oxford University Press, 1965), pp. 19–23. I have proposed some further distinctions in *The Limits of Obligation* (New Haven: Yale University Press, 1982), section 6.

13. Merit is endorsed not only by opponents of preferential treatment but also by many of its supporters. See, for example, Brief of the N.A.A.C.P. Legal Defense and Education Fund as Amicus Curiae, DeFunis v. Odegaard, 416 U.S. 312 (1974), pp. 4–7; Brief of the National Council of Jewish Women and Others as Amici Curiae, *DeFunis*, pp. 66–67; Brief of the City of Seattle as Amicus Curiae, *DeFunis*, pp. 18–20. For a more general discussion, see Allan P. Sindler, *Bakke, DeFunis, and Minority Admissions* (New York: Longman, 1978), chapters 7 and 8.

14. Alan Goldman, *Justice and Reverse Discrimination* (Princeton: Princeton University Press, 1979), p. 22.

15. Both arguments can be found in Rawls, *Theory of Justice*, pp. 66–86, and in Goldman, *Justice and Reverse Discrimination*, pp. 24–34. For an argument that efficiency considerations should have priority and that this priority restricts the application of the merit principle to agglomerations of job assignments that are maximally productive ("positions" in our definition thus being interpreted broadly), see Norman Daniels, "Merit and Meritocracy," *Philosophy and Public Affairs* 7, no. 3 (Spring 1978): 206–23.

16. See Rawls, *Theory of Justice*, p. 73; Williams, "The Idea of Equality," pp. 120–31; and John H. Schaar, "Equality of Opportunity, and Beyond" in J. Roland Pennock and John W. Chapman, eds., *Nomos IX Equality* (New York: Atherton Press, 1967), pp. 228–50.

We can begin with this definition:

THE PRINCIPLE OF MERIT: *There should be widespread proce-dural fairness in the evaluation of qualifications for posi-tions.*

The notion of "procedural fairness," built into the principle of merit, should be distinguished from the deeper issues of "background fairness" in the structure of conditions under which the competition takes place. The latter notion will lead us, as noted already, to equal life chances. Brian Barry usefully illuminates the distinction between these two senses of fair-ness:

Procedural fairness rules out one boxer having a piece of lead inside his gloves, but background fairness would also rule out any undue disparity in the weight of the boxers; similarly background fairness would rule out sailing boats or cars of different sizes being raced against one another unless suitably handicapped. In a court case the fact that one side's counsel showed far greater skill would be grounds for complaint under the rubric of background fairness but not procedural fairness.[17]

A fair competition, I believe, has certain aspects of proce-dural fairness captured by the principle of merit. Yet without conditions of background fairness as well—laying down ground rules for the acquisition of the characteristics people are to *bring* to the competition—procedural fairness would be insufficient. Some of the competitors might never have a chance to develop the required skills and qualifications. When that is the case, there is a serious deficiency in background fairness.

The details of the above definition of merit deserve com-ment. "Positions" can be interpreted as individual job assign-ments which carry with them payoffs in any of the value

17. Barry, *Political Argument*, pp. 98–99.

schemes discussed in the last section. Or, positions can be interpreted more broadly as agglomerations of individual job assignments that would be ranked similarly in any such scheme of value. By "widespread," I mean something approaching universality throughout the society. "Procedural fairness" is more complicated; for the moment, however, we may identify the general notion as those processes that approach the model of an impartial competition. Persons are to be selected for certain characteristics regarded as relevant. For the moment, let us call them "qualifications." Other irrelevant characteristics are, so far as possible (within reasonable limits of cost, time, and effort), to be insulated from affecting the choice. Of course, this does not mean that every job in society has to be subjected to formal competition. Informal processes may strive for, and achieve, procedural fairness in this sense as fully as more formal methods (that is, by choosing those most qualified who would have been selected in a formal competition). The familiar notion of a formal and impartial competition provides a model against which other more informal processes can be assessed.

By "qualifications," I mean criteria that are job-related in that they fairly can be interpreted as indicators of competence or motivation for an individual's performance in a given position. Education, job history, fairly administered test results, or other tokens of ability or effort might all be included.

I assume, furthermore, that criteria for qualifications can be developed for each position, which permit rankings of applicants for that position. In other words, the analogue of a fair competition, determined for the most part by the skill and effort of applicants, holds for each position.

Some aspects of what might be meant by a "fair assessment" of qualifications require little discussion. A fair assessment is, of course, both unbiased and objective. The latter notion might be interpreted to mean that fair assessments must maintain some reasonable degree of inter-subjective reliability. But there is, in addition, another aspect of the fair assessment of qualifications that deserves more comment. I assume that a fair assessment of an individual's qualifications must rest, crucially, on his *own* past or present *actual performance* of relevant tasks, for example, exams, previous employment, or other relevant experience. Therefore, a determination of qualifications should not rest simply on statistical inferences (derived from the behavior of others) about how one might expect a given person to perform. Such a loose determination of qualifications could be stretched to include clearly irrelevant factors such as race or sex if it turned out to be the case that mere membership in a given race or sex statistically predicted performance in a given job. Because of systematic inequalities in developmental conditions, this might certainly turn out to be the case under some empirical conditions. It is important, however, that the principle of merit should not be extended so as to codify such inequalities between groups. Not only would such an extension serve to perpetuate the injustice of the unequal developmental conditions (that is, those that support the statistical inference), but it would also constitute an interpretation of qualifications that is manifestly unfair. An individual in a given group who is subjected to "statistical discrimination,"[18] in this way, would never have had a chance to compete, to prove his own competence. He would be judged entirely on the basis of the performance of *other* persons— persons who happen to share some arbitrary characteristic with him (or her). For this reason, I will assume that a fair assessment of an individual's qualifications must be based, crucially, on that individual's past or present actual performance of relevant tasks.

This interpretation is supported not only by considerations of procedural fairness but also by reasonable interpretations of our basic notion of fair competition. If individuals were assigned to positions without being given the chance to actually

18. I take this term from Lester Thurow, *Generating Inequality* (New York: Basic Books, 1975), pp. 170–81.

perform relevant tasks, in an important sense they would have been denied the chance to compete actively for positions. Having others draw statistical inferences about how they expect you to perform in a competition is not the same as participating in a competition and performing the relevant tasks yourself. For this reason, individuals must be classified according to their actual performance.

This notion of qualifications should generally rule out decisions conforming to the principle of merit that are based on native characteristics such as race, sex, or ethnic origin. It might leave room, however, for a few isolated cases where such a characteristic has a strong contingent association with successful performance in a given job—because of the idiosyncratic character of the tasks involved. In some familiar cases, this contingent association is likely to be so strong that a native characteristic approaches the status of a necessary condition for holding a job. Being female might be considered necessary for modeling certain clothes in the fashion industry. Being male might be necessary for playing tackle in the National Football League. Or consider a looser association. Should being black be considered necessary for the job of teaching Afro-American studies? While many would hold that it should not be considered a qualification, in itself, it is likely to be strongly associated with other characteristics—such as sympathy and experience with the culture to be taught—and most successful applicants for such a position might, justifiably, be black. Nevertheless, so long as race is not, itself, made a decisive qualification, it would be theoretically possible for other applicants to compete successfully.

In cases where the contingent association is so strong that membership in a given race, sex, or religion amounts to a necessary condition for successfully performing a given job (as defined in that society) and as long as such cases are idiosyncratic and isolated, they would not bear on the major issue. The principle of merit, in other words, need not apply to every single position if its application is widespread throughout the society. A few isolated cases of nonmeritocratic assignment would not be worrisome, particularly if those excluded from competing for a given position have an abundance of comparably attractive alternatives they can compete for.

On the other hand, when tasks are *commonly* defined so that arbitrary native characteristics are often relevant to the performance of work roles, as so defined, then a challenge to the principle of merit of a quite different kind arises. Suppose that in a given society all the higher positions are presently occupied by white males and that the ability to work effectively, without disruption, with the other occupants of high positions is built into the definition of the tasks required for those positions. In such a society, it would not be difficult to imagine widely accepted ideological tenets differentiating race and sex whereby females and nonwhites introduced into the higher positions would be a disrupting influence (at least for a time). Could such considerations justifiably enter into the definition of the work roles for which people are to compete, according to the principle of merit?

The difficulty is that if qualifications were stretched to include such considerations, certain native characteristics would, de facto, turn out to be decisive in the process of assignment. The definition of "merit" would have been distorted in such a way that certain groups would never really have had a chance to compete for the positions in question. This example points out that an adequate principle of merit must do more than require a fair assessment of the extent to which an individual has acquired certain qualifications. It must also require a fair determination of what are to count as qualifications in the first place.

Recall the definition of qualifications specified above: "criteria that are job-related in that they fairly can be interpreted as indicators of competence or motivation for an individual's performance in a given position." Should a fair interpretation of an individual's competence and motivation to perform in a given position include reference to his or her race, sex, or ethnic origin? Familiar interpretations of the principle of merit would, in fact, hold all such factors to be irrelevant. Some views apply this notion quite strictly so that they must be completely irrelevant to each particular position falling under the principle of merit. Other views would accept "separate but equal" competitions under certain circumstances. For example, while males might not be eligible to model female clothes in the fashion industry, they would be eligible to model male clothes. If the opportunities were truly comparable, the looser interpretations of the principle of merit (those permitting dual competitions) would find such arrangements admissible. Of course, the "separate but equal" doctrine has a notorious history but that is, in large part, because it was employed in contexts where separate clearly was not—and perhaps could never have been—equal.[19] We need not decide this question here. The argument I will develop applies equally to the strict meritocratic doctrine for each single position and to those interpretations that would permit some separate but equal competitions—provided that the parallel opportunities were, in fact, equal.

I leave open the question, in other words, whether separate but truly equal competitions are ever admissible for sexual, racial, or ethnic divisions in the population. I leave this question open because my argument is meant to apply to all of the defensible varieties of the principle of merit; different but plausible versions of the doctrine handle this question in different ways. My hope is that the argument developed here will apply to all of them.

The basic point, however, is that native characteristics should not have any direct role in determining the payoffs any individual can expect from the process of meritocratic assignment. Either such factors should be completely irrelevant or their effect should be ameliorated through parallel but equal

19. See Richard Kluger, *Simple Justice: The History of Brown v. Board of Education and Black America's Struggle for Equality* (New York: Vintage Books, 1977).

competitions. For the moment I will set aside this looser interpretation, permitting the possibility of some parallel competitions, and concentrate on the straightforward case of a unified process of meritocratic assignment regardless of all native characteristics.

There are two aspects of fairness that must be emphasized. The first concerns the assessment of qualifications. The second concerns the determination of standards for that assessment, the determination, in other words, of what are to count as qualifications for a given position. Except where their effect has been ameliorated by equal parallel competitions, native characteristics should not have an explicit role in either process. By a native characteristic, I mean any factor knowable at birth that could be employed to differentiate adult persons of at least normal health and endowment.[20] A person's race, sex, ethnic origin, and family background would all count as native characteristics. Even the purely genetic component of IQ, if it were possible to isolate such a thing, would count as a native characteristic. A ban on considering the purely genetic component of IQ would not rule out considering fully developed IQ which is, of course, influenced by environment as well as by heredity.[21]

The basic idea is that an individual has no responsibility

20. A similar conception of native characteristics is employed by Goldman, *Justice and Reverse Discrimination*, p. 102, for example. However, one of his arguments against considering them in assigning people to positions interprets them as "unalterable characteristics unrelated to performance" (p. 34). Even though native characteristics can be ascribed to an individual at birth, they are not necessarily unalterable, as cases of sex change illustrate dramatically. I have restricted the discussion to persons of normal health and endowment because there are special issues applying to the handicapped—issues of sufficient importance to justify lengthy treatment that would distract from our central argument here. It would hardly be novel to claim that there are difficult controversies applying to equal opportunity for the handicapped. My argument here is directed at establishing the difficulty of equal opportunity for the supposedly easy case of normal persons who have no significant physical or mental handicaps. For discussion of justice involving the handicapped see Goldman, *Justice and Reverse Discrimination*, pp. 180–182 and Susan Rose-Ackerman, "Mental Retardation and Society," forthcoming in *Ethics*.

21. For the current confused state of research on the genetic component of

whatsoever for any of his or her purely native characteristics. Race, sex, family background, or ethnic origin can all be simply ascribed to an individual at birth. It is, therefore, unfair to consider them explicitly in the process of meritocratic assignment, either in the assessment of qualifications or in the determination of what factors are to count as qualifications. They are not factors subject to competitive efforts at acquisition; therefore, it would be unfair to let them determine the competition among talents, as developed. Of course, such factors will usually be ruled out, in any case, since it would be unusual for them to support the justificatory burden of being job-related at least for most of the work roles that are familiar to us. Were work roles to be defined, however, so that such factors became relevant, as in the example of the hierarchical white male system, the above assumption about fairness would prevent them from being considered.

What do I mean by this ban preventing native characteristics from being "considered explicitly" in the process of meritocratic assignment? The qualifications should be defined, and the competition should be run, in such a way that it should always be possible for two persons who differ markedly in any such native characteristics to be judged equally qualified. More precisely, the qualifications should be defined so that a black could change places with a white, a female could change places with a male, or a Jew could change places with a gentile, for example, and no noticeable effect on the assessment of qualifications need arise from the exchange.[22] The evaluation of merit should be blind to such considerations.

Of course, some have advocated sacrificing or abridging the

IQ see Block and Dworkin, *The IQ Controversy*, especially part 2, and H. J. Eysenck and Leon Kamin, *The Intelligence Controversy* (New York: John Wiley & Sons, Inc., 1981).

22. For a more general discussion of this kind of exchange requirement, see my *Limits of Obligation*, section 5. For a similar application to notions of merit, see Goldman, p. 53. For an attack on this admittedly liberal requirement—on the grounds that it ignores differences between the sexes—see Elizabeth H. Wolgast, *Equality and the Rights of Women* (Ithaca: Cornell University Press, 1980), chapter 1.

principle of merit as compensation for past injustice to particular groups. As long as the conflict with merit considerations is explicitly acknowledged, nothing I have said thus far determines, one way or another, whether such practices would be justifiable. I will return to this question later.[23] For the moment, it is worth noting that my argument about the necessity for sacrificing the principle of merit under certain conditions will take place, by contrast, within the ground rules of ideal theory. My argument is that the principle of merit conflicts irreconcilably with other core liberal assumptions under the best conditions that might realistically be imagined for a modern industrial society. While liberal theorists might be resigned to sacrifices in the principle of merit as compensation for past injustice, there is a much more disturbing challenge to liberal theories of justice, I believe, in the requirement for such sacrifices under *ideal* conditions. As one corner of the trilemma to be explored later, the principle of merit is, indeed, placed in such jeopardy.

2.3 Equality of Life Chances

While the principle of merit has usually been accepted as a necessary part of an adequate account of equal opportunity (at least under favorable conditions),[24] it is vulnerable to some obvious objections when applied by itself. There are cases when the principle of merit could be fully implemented and we would all be fairly sure that equal opportunity, in any meaningful sense, had not been achieved.

Consider this example which I have adopted from Bernard Williams.[25] Imagine a society dominated by a warrior class—a society where the top positions are all occupied by skillful warriors who have perpetuated their positions from one generation to the next. Suppose, however, that advocates of equal

---

23. See sections 3.7 and 4.3 below.
24. See Goldman, *Justice and Reverse Discrimination*, chapter 2. See also, n. 5, chapter 1 above.
25. Williams, "The Idea of Equality," p. 126.

opportunity institute a reform. They decide that admission to the warrior class should, from that point on, be determined by a suitable competition.

As it happens, however, the present warriors' children over-whelmingly dominate the competition so that the reform makes no difference in the outcome. We might imagine, for example, that children of the warrior class are all well nourished while their competitors are so undernourished that they fail in the competition for lack of strength. Any reason-able witness to the spectacle of 300 pound wrestlers vanquish-ing 90 pound weaklings would conclude that an inadequate and merely procedural kind of equal opportunity had been realized by the reform. Nevertheless, it should be noted that the winners of the competition would, undoubtedly, be better warriors. Choosing them would be fully compatible with the principle of merit; our dissatisfaction with the reform has to do with the unequal causal conditions under which merit— namely the characteristics measured in the competition—has developed. In an important sense, children of the lower strata never really would have had a suitable chance to win the competition because they never really would have had a suit-able chance to develop the valued characteristics.

Suppose, however, that children of the warrior class all win, not because they are better fed, but because their parents have helped them develop the appropriate skills. They are, indeed, better warriors, but because of parental influence rather than because of superior nourishment. If one could predict the outcome of the competition, just as reliably, by reference to family background, then the institution of a procedurally fair competition still would appear inadequate as an account of equal opportunity. It would merely institutionalize grossly unequal life chances. The basic intuition is that it seems unfair that we should be able to predict eventual positions in a society merely by knowing the strata into which children are born. If that is the case, then we may say that the initial distribution of life chances is unacceptably unequal. In this case, it is unequal because of identifiable and remediable causal conditions which differentially affect the development of qualifications in the first place.

It is worth adding that we might object to such grossly unequal life chances whether or not they came about through differential opportunities for talent development. If the top stratum were not composed of more skillful warriors, but constituted, instead, a hereditary aristocracy that perpetuated its control over important positions in the society—without any special claim to skill or expertise—then, surely, the result would be at least equally objectionable. Differential life chances could, in this case, be predicted just as easily on the basis of the stratum one was born into. The fact that the top stratum was mediocre in its talents would only provide further grounds for criticizing the system.

Let us define the root notion operating in these objections:

EQUALITY OF LIFE CHANCES: *The prospects of children for eventual positions in society should not vary in any systematic and significant manner with their arbitrary native characteristics.*

By "prospects," I mean the probability of reaching given positions, as that probability might be impartially and objectively assessed. By "positions," I mean here any scheme of ranking social outcomes or job assignments. Any such scheme can be thought of as an answer to the questions I identified in section 2.1 under the problem of value (in theories of distributive justice). Positions might, in other words, be ranked in terms of income, utility, social esteem, Rawlsian primary goods, or other such theories.

What do I mean by "arbitrary" native characteristics? A native characteristic will be considered arbitrary unless it predicts the development of qualifications to a high degree among children who have been subjected to equal developmental conditions.[26] Hence if IQ or even height turned out to be

26. Of course, there are many dimensions along which equal developmental conditions might be measured. Some versions of equal environmental conditions will reveal dramatic differences while others will not. J. M. Thoday cites

major qualifications of job relevance in a given society, knowing the genetic component of such factors at birth might
permit one to predict the differential development of qualifications—even among persons whose environmental conditions
had been fully equalized. But unless a native characteristic
withstands this justificatory burden of predicting the development of qualifications under equal conditions, it will be considered morally irrelevant to the development of qualifications
and, hence, arbitrary. Thus race, sex, ethnic origin, family
background, and other such familiar dimensions of discrimination will be considered arbitrary here. Under equal developmental conditions, I will assume that knowledge of these
factors would not permit us to reliably predict qualifications of
individuals for desirable positions in the society. Inequalities
in the qualifications achieved by these groups, I will assume,
can be traced to differential developmental conditions.[27]

----

some interesting experiments involving plants. When two distinct genotypes
of goldenrod are both subjected to the same high light intensity, their development is indistinguishable. But when they are both subjected to the same low
light intensity dramatic differences ensue. Clearly, the choice between different versions of equal developmental conditions may be crucial. See J. M.
Thoday, "Limitations to Genetic Comparison of Populations," in Block and
Dworkin, *The IQ Controversy*, pp. 131–45.
    27. Relaxing this assumption, and treating these inequalities between
groups (defined along racial, ethnic, or class lines) as genetic (rather than
environmental) is of course, another theoretical possibility. The controversies
recently generated by Jensen and Herrnstein arose from their bringing into
question the assumption made here (Jensen along racial lines, Herrnstein along
class divisions in a meritocracy). I will not enter into this controversial and
unsettled empirical issue here. Rather, my strategy will be to employ the
optimistic and quintessentially liberal assumption that there are *no* systematic genetic differences between groups (defined along racial, ethnic, or class
divisions) that would bear on meritocratic assignment. Based on this, my
argument in chapter three can be read as a claim that even *if* this optimistic
empirical assumption is employed, the trilemma of equal opportunity is
unavoidable. Clearly, the conflict between merit and equal life chances would
only be exacerbated if the Jensen or Herrnstein theses were correct. For then,
even *with* equalization of developmental conditions (accomplished through
sacrifice of family autonomy), equal life chances could not be achieved with
the principle of merit in place. Membership in the allegedly genetically
superior or inferior group would predict differential development of competence even under equal developmental conditions. Hence, it would predict

Hence, by the principle of equal life chances, if I can predict the outcomes achieved by an individual merely by knowing his or her race, sex, ethnic origin, or family background, then equality of life chances has not been realized.

It may seem odd that some native characteristics, nonarbitrary ones, are strictly insulated from the process of meritocratic assignment but are not, similarly, insulated from the distribution of equal life chances. For example, the purely genetic component of IQ, were it possible to measure it with confidence, could not, by itself, constitute a qualification relevant to the principle of merit. IQ, as fully developed, on the other hand, would be admissible, as would any other measures of cognitive skills that were job-related. We have already explored a variety of reasons for this conclusion. One reason arises directly from the fairness requirement, introduced earlier: A fair assessment of an individual's qualifications must rest, crucially, on his own past or present actual performance of relevant tasks, for example, exams, previous employment, or other relevant experience. Obviously, any native characteristic (that must, by definition, be ascertainable at birth) could not count directly as a qualification in this sense, since it would not depend on an individual's actual performance of any relevant tasks. The future ability to perform such a task, however, would be a different matter.

Why, on the other hand, should the principle of equal life chances not be formulated, similarly, so as to insulate the distribution of life chances from all such native characteristics (and not merely the arbitrary ones)? We might envision a possible formulation of the principle that would have this effect—namely, that persons should have equal life chances

---

differential life chances (because of differing competence) with the principle of merit in place. This kind of argument would require not only (a) the controversial genetic differences between groups and (b) the high heritability of the relevant factors, but also (c) meritocratic assignment in the society according to precisely those factors that conform to (a) and (b). Even if the controversial claims alleged for IQ were established (a and b), the substantial role of many *other* cognitive and personality factors in any plausible system of meritocratic

regardless of whether they are born more or less talented (or with greater or lesser genetic components of the relevant talents). I have not formulated the principle in this way because the version of the principle that has had greatest appeal has been more concerned with the equalization of life chances across differing environments than across differing genetic endowments. The idea has been to equalize chances for natural talents to flourish rather than to equalize chances regardless of natural talents.

I mention this kind of more demanding principle to note that the argument of the next chapter applies equally to it. Our definition of equal life chances could easily be adapted to yield such a requirement. Such a principle would simply regard all native characteristics as arbitrary—including those clearly relevant to the development of talents under equal conditions. This principle would be far more demanding in that it would equalize life chances not only for all the cases treated by our proposal (across sectors of society, ethnic groups, sexual and racial divisions), but also across differing natural endowments of the relevant talents. Given the difficulties we will encounter with the weaker version of the principle in the required manipulation of developmental conditions, I note the stronger one only in passing as a more demanding version that produces the same trilemma but that has other implications as well.

2.4 The Autonomy of the Family The third assumption is defined as follows:

AUTONOMY OF THE FAMILY: *Consensual relations within a given family governing the development of its children*

assignment would be enough to throw the issue open again. See Block and Dworkin, *The IQ Controversy;* Arthur R. Jensen, *Educability and Group Differences* (London: Methuen, 1973); R. J. Herrnstein, *IQ in the Meritocracy* (Boston: Little Brown, 1973). For a sampling of the storm of protest raised by Jensen's thesis, see *Environment, Heredity, and Intelligence,* compiled from the *Harvard Educational Review,* reprint series, 2 (Cambridge: Harvard Educational Review, 1969).

should not be coercively interfered with except to ensure for the children the essential prerequisites for adult participation in the society.

By "essential prerequisites," I mean the physical and psychological health of the child and his or her knowledge of those social conventions necessary for participation in adult society. Literacy, the routines of citizenship, and other familiar elements of secondary education would count among the essential prerequisites. Hence, parents who failed to ensure such prerequisites for their children could justifiably be subject to state interference.[28]

By a "family," I mean here "a community composed of a child and one or more adults in a close affective and physical relation which is expected to endure at least through childhood."[29] Such a family may be more extended than the familiar nuclear one and it need not, for purposes of this broad definition, include two parents of opposite sex. I assume, however, that natural parents have the initial option of *creating* families (subject to this principle) if they do so in a consensual manner, that is, one not subject to sustained and intense disagreement. Hence this definition leaves open questions about the appropriate role of the state when there is sufficient disagreement (non-consensual relations) between natural parents over who should be included in a given family. In other words, this principle is not intended to resolve questions of child custody when parents disagree, nor is it intended to resolve questions of child placement when neither of the parents wants the

28. I leave open the question of criteria for justified intervention in such cases falling outside the area of family autonomy protected by the principle stated here. The ever present possibility of the child suffering more harm than good from government interventions that disrupt the continuity of family relations should be emphasized. See Joseph Goldstein, Anna Freud, and Albert J. Solnit, *Beyond the Best Interests of the Child* (New York: Free Press, 1973) and *Before the Best Interests of the Child* (New York: Free Press, 1979).

29. John E. Coons and Stephen D. Sugarman, *Education by Choice: The Case for Family Control* (Berkeley: University of California Press, 1978), p. 53.

child.[30] Similarly, this definition is not intended to resolve questions about "children's rights" when consensual relations between adults and children break down to the point, for example, that a child wishes to be placed in another family or in an institution.[31]

Rather, this definition is directed at cases where the state might wish to interfere in a family that preserves consensual relations—where there is not sustained and intense disagreement about its basic terms of cooperation. This principle would give parents considerable latitude in influencing the development of their children, in a manner preserving consensus within the family, as long as provision of the essential prerequisites for adult participation in the society were not endangered.[32]

Furthermore, by limiting the autonomy principle to matters bearing on child development, I mean to define the principle narrowly so as to avoid the most obvious and controversial areas of conflict with the principle of merit. Most importantly, family autonomy is not meant to govern job assignments in adult society. It should not be construed to protect nepotism, the buying of positions, or large-scale inheritance. Such practices would raise obvious conflicts with any attempts to fully institutionalize merit. My argument will require only a narrow and comparatively noncontroversial construction of family

30. See Goldstein et al., *Beyond the Best Interests*, part 2.

31. See Goldstein et al., *Before the Best Interests*, chapter 7; Beatrice Gross and Ronald Gross, eds., *The Children's Rights Movement* (New York: Anchor Press/Doubleday, 1977); and Patricia Vardin and Ilene N. Brody, eds., *Children's Rights: Contemporary Perspectives* (New York: Teacher's College Press, 1979).

32. For a basically similar position, maintaining that the autonomy of intact families should not be interfered with, except when extreme harm to the child is in question, see Goldstein et al., *Before the Best Interests*, chapters 1 and 2. See also Laurence D. Houlgate, *The Child and the State: A Normative Theory of Juvenile Rights* (Baltimore: Johns Hopkins, 1980). Houlgate's arguments protecting paternalism within the family, along with his arguments for positive and negative claim rights protecting children from various forms of harm and abuse, are compatible with the principle developed here.

autonomy. As defined here, the principle protects only the core of parent-child relations, namely, consensual efforts to influence child development.

What do I mean by "coercive interference" in this definition of the autonomy principle? A person (or group), X, attempts to coercively interfere with the actions of a person (or group), Y, if X attempts to direct Y to choose one alternative course of action, A, rather than other courses, B, C, D, and so on, by either (i) threatening Y with disadvantages he would not otherwise encounter if he fails to choose A, or (ii) by systematically suppressing knowledge or discussion of the alternatives to action A (or the favorable aspects of those alternatives) with the intention of directing Y to choose A.[33]

Hence, if the state threatens nonconforming families with imprisonment or loss of custody of their children, that would clearly constitute coercive interference. Such coercive interference would, as noted, be justified in some cases in order to ensure a child's education or essential aspects of his physical or psychological health. Or, if the government were to manipulate behavior by suppressing discussion and knowledge of all alternatives but certain approved paths, that would also constitute coercive interference.

It is worth noting that this principle is a relatively weak one. The protection it offers from coercive interference does not apply whenever consensual relations in a family are lacking or whenever the essential prerequisites for adult participation are in serious question for a given child. It would protect the family from interference only when these common grounds for

33. For an account of coercion generally similar to the first clause in this definition, see Robert Nozick, "Coercion," in Peter Laslett, W. G. Runciman, and Quentin Skinner, *Philosophy, Politics and Society, Fourth Series* (Oxford: Basil Blackwell, 1972), pp. 101–35. Unlike Nozick, however, I would consistently treat omissions that would be intentionally and causally connected to someone being made worse-off as "threats." Nozick ("Coercion," p. 115) leaves the question open, as in the case of P (in a rowboat) refusing to save Q (in the water) from drowning. The second clause of this definition has an independent basis; it relies on the notion that brainwashing and indoctrination violate liberty coercively just as effectively as might force or the threat of force.

justified interference are both lacking. It thus attempts to single out the least controversial portion of the sphere of action within which families might claim autonomy from coercive interference.

Not only is this principle appealing in its own right but it can also be supported within a broader framework of negative liberty. While this extension is not, strictly speaking, essential for the main argument below, it does help identify the stakes at issue were the autonomy of the family to be intruded upon. According to some important notions in the liberal tradition, protection for the family is embedded within a broader conception of negative liberty. While I will employ the precise assumption defined above, liberals who are committed to the broader framework of negative liberty will find a crucial portion of that framework at risk in the argument below. The autonomy of the family assumption defined above identifies that portion of negative liberty which touches most of our lives most directly.

It has long been a central concern of the liberal tradition that there be a significant sphere where a person, in Berlin's words "should be left to do or be what he is able to do or be, without interference by other persons."[34] Much liberal thinking on the definition of this sphere has been influenced by Mill's "harm principle"—his "one very simple principle" in *On Liberty*.

> That principle is that the sole end for which mankind are warranted, individually or collectively, in interfering with the liberty of action of any of their number is self protection. That the only purpose for which power can be rightfully exercised over any member of a civilized community, against his will, is to prevent harm to others.[35]

34. Isaiah Berlin, *Four Essays on Liberty* (Oxford: Oxford University Press, 1969), pp. 121–22.
35. John Stuart Mill, *On Liberty*, (New York: Bobbs-Merrill, 1956), p. 13. I take the term "harm principle" from Joel Feinberg's influential discussion in *Social Philosophy*, (Englewood Cliffs, N.J.: Prentice-Hall, 1973), chapters 2 and 3.

The sphere of what Mill calls "self-regarding" action should thus be immune from interference precisely because, by definition, it does not harm others. Regardless of whether Mill's principle is taken in the strong sense he proposes, namely, as stating the necessary (and perhaps sufficient) conditions for justified interferences with liberty, it can usefully be employed to identify an essential part of the justified sphere of liberty.[36] Mill's principle offers a powerful and appealing position: acts that do not harm others should be immune from coercive interference. As Mill describes this self-regarding area of life:

> there is a sphere of action in which society, as distinguished from the individual, has, if any, only an indirect interest: comprehending all that portion of a person's life and conduct which affects only himself or, if it also affects others, only with their free voluntary, and undeceived consent and participation.[37]

Yet this position, as formulated, applies only to those "in the maturity of their faculties." Its application to children is left unclear. Mill's comments about children later in the essay suggest how the general framework might be extended. First, with respect to education:

> It still remains unrecognized, that to bring a child into existence without a fair prospect of being able, not only to provide food for its body, but instruction and training for its mind, is a moral crime, both against the unfortunate offspring and against society; and that if the parent does not fulfill this obligation, the State ought to see it fulfilled, at the charge, as far as possible, of the parent.[38]

36. For criticism that Mill's principle may cover only a tiny sphere of action, depending on how the causation of harm is construed, see Richard Taylor, *Freedom, Anarchy and the Law* (Englewood Cliffs, N.J.: Prentice-Hall, 1973), chapter 9. For a more sympathetic interpretation, see Feinberg, *Social Philosophy*, chapters 2 and 3.

37. Mill, *On Liberty*, pp. 15–16.

38. Ibid., p. 128. The caveat limiting the principle to persons "in the maturity of their faculties" appears on p. 13.

Hence, the state may require that children be educated up to a certain standard and this coercive interference, when necessary, is justified in order to prevent severe harm both to the child and to others in society at large.

A similar extension of the harm principle can be applied to the initial act of creating a new human being:

> The fact itself, of causing the existence of a new human being, is one of the most responsible actions in the range of human action. To undertake this responsibility—to bestow a life which may be either a curse or a blessing—unless the being on whom it will be bestowed will have at least the ordinary chances of a desirable existence, is a crime against that being.[39]

Under certain conditions of overpopulation or scarcity, production of a new human being may be coercively regulated in order to prevent harm to the one conceived (and to others). While there are many interesting questions about the conceptualization of harm to possible persons,[40] this interference might be interpreted as resting on a claim that there are some conditions under which it would have been better for a person not to have been born at all. Under such deprivating conditions, one is, in effect, harming a person by bringing him into existence to lead such a life.[41]

For both these issues—education and procreation—the self-regarding framework of the harm principle can be extended to include regulation by the state of parental actions when sufficient harm to the child is in question. Here children are

39. Ibid., p. 132.

40. See Sikora and Barry, *Obligations to Future Generations*; Derek Parfit, "On Doing the Best for our Children," in Michael Bayles, ed., *Ethics and Population* (Cambridge: Schenkman, 1976), pp. 100–18; and Jeff McMahan, "Problems of Population Theory," *Ethics* 92, no. 1 (October 1981): 96–127.

41. See McMahan, "Problems of Population Theory," part 7, and Jan Narveson, "Future People and Us," in Sikora and Barry, eds., *Obligations to Future Generations*, pp. 38–60, especially pp. 47–48. Recall the Yiddish joke cited by Nozick (*Anarchy*, p. 337): "Life is so terrible it would be better never to have been conceived. Yes but who is so fortunate? Not one in a thousand."

included among the others, in the phrase "prevent harm to others," as the motivation for justified government interference.

So children can be incorporated into the protected self-regarding sphere among consenting adults provided that due care is taken to ensure that they are not significantly harmed as a result. It is worth noting that this protected self-regarding sphere is much broader than the area of negative liberty involved in our argument. For as defined, it would include public consensual acts that affect others as in the phrase "an affecting sight."[42] Displays of pornography around Times Square might be protected within the sphere defined so broadly. While a good case can be made for the protection of such behavior,[43] it adds further controversy to the argument and need not be defended here. So let us single out a less controversial *portion* of the self-regarding sphere of liberty as follows:

THE PRIVATE SPHERE OF LIBERTY: *So long as no one is severely harmed, intimate consensual relations should be immune from coercive interference.*

By "intimate" relations, I mean those personal interactions that are both private and affective. By "private," I mean interactions that require the option of privacy in that their character would be changed if they were coercively subjected to public scrutiny and/or interference. The option of privacy, in other words, is part of the freedom of interaction that would be protected by this principle.

Relations between adults and children in a given family are among the intimate consensual relations protected by this private sphere of liberty. The latter is broader, of course, in that intimate relations in addition to family relations would be protected by it as well.[44] It would not be an exaggeration,

42. See Brian Barry, *Political Argument*, pp. 63–64, 71–72.
43. David A. J. Richards, *The Moral Criticism of Law* (Encino, Calif.: Dickenson Publishing Co., 1977), chapter 3.
44. See, for example, the classic debate between Hart and Devlin. H. L. A.

however, to conclude that the portion of the private sphere of liberty that is least controversial and of greatest importance to most of us is, without doubt, the part singled out by the autonomy of the family. Hence, it is this portion that I will employ in my argument below. Were this portion of the private sphere of liberty to be sacrificed, the realm of negative liberty remaining would be mutilated virtually beyond recognition.

The argument in the following chapter could be formulated either in terms of the autonomy of the family or in terms of the broader claim defined by the private sphere of liberty. And the violations of the autonomy of the family to be investigated there must also be violations of the private sphere of liberty.[45] Because the narrower principle is less controversial, however, and because it also identifies the issues at stake more precisely, I will employ it. It brings into sharper focus the conflicts between conventional morality and systematic liberal theory and, hence, will lead us more easily into the methodological issues to be raised later in the book in chapter 5.

Hart, *Law, Liberty and Morality* (Oxford: Oxford University Press, 1963), and Patrick Devlin, *The Enforcement of Morals* (Oxford: Oxford University Press, 1965).

45. In other words, the consensual relations between adults and children protected by the autonomy of the family assumption are *among* the intimate consensual relations protected by the private sphere of liberty. Lack of the "essential prerequisites" in the former principle can be treated as the kind of "severe harm" mentioned in the latter. Provided that we restrict the discussion to harms involving children, the acts protected by family autonomy would all be protected by the broader principle of the private sphere of liberty.

3. THE TRILEMMA OF
EQUAL OPPORTUNITY

The three principles just de-fined combine to form a tri-lemma—realization of any two can be expected to preclude realization of the third. The resulting options are each disturbing in that each involves a systematic and severe sacrifice in one of the three principles. Before proceeding to develop this argument, some ground rules for the discussion should be established.

3.1 Ideal Theory

Let us embark upon the some-what utopian task of imagining the best possible conditions that might realistically obtain in a modern industrial society, both in terms of objective economic and social circumstances and in terms of human cooperation. Following Rawls, let us say that there is only "moderate scarcity" in this society and that there is "strict compliance" with principles of justice. In this dual sense, Rawls's characterization of the problem of "ideal theory" provides a useful starting point.[1] Later, we will have reason to

1. I take the term "ideal theory" from Rawls, *Theory of Justice*, p. 245. "Strict compliance" refers to support for *institutional* choices (and their corresponding principles); it does not carry with it universal compliance with every act of *individual* choice (and behavior) that institutions might prescribe for their citizens. The latter, more ambitious assumption would render the argument clearly utopian. Suppose, for example, that we were simply to assume that every individual worked as hard as he does now, despite a perfectly equalizing tax system, because policymakers would like the norm of social duty contributions to become widely accepted in the society. To interpret strict compliance so broadly as to yield universal conformity to all the hypothesized individual choices would be to beg all the interesting issues

discuss critically his particular proposals for our central problem of equal opportunity.

By "moderate scarcity" Rawls means:

Natural and other resources are not so abundant that schemes of cooperation become superfluous, nor are conditions so harsh that fruitful ventures must inevitably break down. While mutually advantageous arrangements are feasible, the benefits they yield fall short of the demands men put forward.[2]

In other words, the question of justice arises under these admittedly favorable conditions because conflicting demands cannot be fully satisfied; yet this degree of scarcity is far from extreme. This might be specified further as some assumption that conditions well beyond subsistence are possible for everyone in the society.

This condition of moderate scarcity still requires some further specification to be useful for our purposes. I will interpret it as imposing what might be called a *realistic budget constraint*. Resources are not unlimited; the resources devoted to any particular worthy goal must compete with other legitimate demands. In the next few sections I will focus on only a part of the question of justice—the issue of assignment. There are other components of the theory of justice and other legitimate moral demands quite apart from those specified by the theory of distributive justice. Hence, while the resources devoted to implementing any of the principles discussed below may be substantial, they must compete with other legitimate demands—health care, national defense, care for the aged, environmental protection, international redistribution or foreign aid, and a viable and fair system of criminal justice (the

---

about the realistic possibilities for such a proposal (incentive effects, indoctrination, and so forth). Hence, strict compliance will be interpreted in terms of institutional choice. Realistic problems of enforcing individual conformity would still have to be faced within ideal theory as thus defined.

2. Ibid., p. 127.

latter falls within retributive rather than distributive justice). Improvements in the realization of our three principles might be worth sacrifices in any of these other worthy goals. Such improvements, however, would not merit substantially sacrificing all of them.[3] There are, in other words, certain outer limits on the resources that can be devoted to any of our three principles, limits set by the fact that the government and other social institutions face a host of other legitimate moral demands that are separable from the particular policy area we are focusing on here, the issue of assignment. These limits constitute a realistic budget constraint. While they are vague at the level of general application necessary for our argument, they will permit us to rule out some proposals as clearly unrealistic or utopian because their prohibitive expense would surpass any realistic construction of the budget constraint. For example, it would violate such a constraint to supply every student in society his own full-time team of elite private tutors comparable to the best talent available in private education.[4] Provided that our use of the budget constraint is limited largely to ruling out such clearly fantastic examples, its admitted vagueness will not affect the development of our argument.

In addition to moderate scarcity, let us assume "strict compliance": "Everyone is presumed to act justly and to do his part in upholding just institutions."[5] More specifically, we might suppose that there is good will, cooperation, and conscientious agreement on implementing the principles under discussion. Furthermore, we might assume that such good will is not only operative at the time principles are implemented but that it has also been characteristic of the relevant recent history. This would conform to Rawls's assumption that "strict compliance theory" does not have to deal with questions of "compensatory" justice.[6]

3. The argument below will require only the acceptance of some general upper limit. Because we will employ it only to rule out certain clearly utopian proposals, its admitted vagueness will not affect the argument.

4. See section 3.6 below.

5. Rawls, *Theory of Justice*, p. 8.

6. Ibid.

This notion of strict compliance will structure certain ground rules in the argument below. My claim will be that achievement of any two principles realistically precludes achievement of the third. Hence, I will assume in this argument that the two principles under discussion have been conscientiously implemented not only at the time of discussion, but also in the relevant recent history. In addition, I will assume that the remaining principle has also been the subject of conscientious effort and cooperation within the limits resulting from the comparatively more successful efforts to implement the other two.

These conditions, moderate scarcity and strict compliance, rule out some of the more obvious cases under which a serious sacrifice in one or more of our three principles might be acceptable. For example, under conditions of extreme (rather than merely moderate) scarcity, it is commonly granted that the private sphere of liberty might have to be seriously infringed upon in order to regulate population growth. Similarly, when there has not been a history of strict compliance, but rather, a legacy of injustice to specific groups, such as American blacks or native Americans, there is a compensatory argument that could not otherwise arise for abridging the principle of merit. Lastly, when instead of strict compliance, there is organized opposition from entrenched power groups, it is possible that attempts to equalize life chances might not be worth the costs of reform. While each of these sacrifices in one of our three principles might be understandable and necessary under the conditions of non-ideal theory, they would constitute a more disturbing challenge to liberal assumptions if they were required under the ideal conditions of both strict compliance and only moderate scarcity. The general argument that follows will confine itself to such ideal conditions.

3.2 Background Inequalities   Throughout the modern world, equality is generally prescribed, yet inequality is generally practiced. Assertions of moral equality lie at the root of all the ideologies commonly accepted in the developed countries.[7] Yet all of these countries, whether capitalist or socialist, whether democratic or hierarchical (or some hybrid combination of these) have very substantial economic and social inequalities. Some of the state socialist systems of Eastern Europe have, at times, made impressive gains in equalizing opportunities across class barriers. Nevertheless, they remain highly stratified economically and socially.[8] Similarly, no proposals for redistribution that have been seriously entertained in any of the Western capitalist systems would come remotely close to equalizing outcomes.[9] The deprivations of poverty at the bottom might be reduced by such proposals and inequalities might be limited somewhat; they would not, however, be eliminated.

Traditional societies, furthermore, have rarely been distinguished by any substantial degree of equality—economic or social. Rather, they have only been more forthright in their acceptance of inequality. They have more explicitly matched inegalitarian ideologies to highly stratified outcomes.[10]

7. See Douglas Rae et al., *Equalities* (Cambridge: Harvard University Press, 1981), and Sanford Lakoff, *Equality in Political Philosophy* (Cambridge: Harvard University Press, 1964).

8. Charles E. Lindblom, *Politics and Markets: The World's Politico-Economic Systems* (New York: Basic Books, 1977), chapter 20. See also David Lane, *The End of Inequality? Stratification under State Socialism* (Harmondsworth, Eng.: Penguin Book, 1971), and Frank Parkin, *Class Inequality and Political Order* (New York: Praeger, 1971). For claims about progress in equal opportunity in state socialist systems, see Parkin, chapter 5, especially section 4.

9. See, for example, Arthur M. Okun, *Equality and Efficiency: The Big Tradeoff* (Washington, D.C.: The Brookings Institution, 1975), chapter 4, and Lindblom, *Politics and Markets*, chapter 3. For an admittedly utopian but more strictly egalitarian proposal, see Joseph H. Carens, *Equality, Moral Incentives and the Market: An Essay in Utopian Politico-Economic Theory* (Chicago: University of Chicago Press, 1981). Carens, however, self-consciously avoids the problem of "transition" from the present American policy context to his utopian system. It is not, in other words, offered as a program we might now try to implement. It is limited to the important questions of ideal theory. See section 4.4 below.

10. See, for example, Barrington Moore, Jr., *Injustice: The Social Bases of*

If any modern economy must organize itself either through the use of market incentives or through the use of command or hierarchy, it should be clear that substantial inequalities, both economic and social, always accompany both of these basic mechanisms. Hybrid systems, furthermore, have never offered any escape from the problem. Large-scale experiments with market socialism, on the one hand, and democratic socialism, on the other, have always, whatever their other merits, been subject to the same charge.[11]

The division of labor necessary for a complex, technologically advanced economy may, itself, provide one of the root causes of both economic and social inequality. For it may carry with it a host of social, psychological, and economic differentiations that provide the basis for a hierarchy of status or esteem. Such advanced economies may also require economic differentiations to support the necessary investments in skill and training and to motivate performance. Even those socialist systems (in less developed countries) that have attempted to replace economic incentives with "moral" ones have introduced social inequalities as a result.[12]

These observations all support my assumption, in the argument that follows, that any large-scale modern industrial society will have substantial social and economic inequalities. In

---

Obedience and Revolt (White Plains, N.Y.: M. E. Sharpe, 1978), and Louis Dumont, *Homo Hierarchicus: The Caste System and Its Implications* (Chicago: University of Chicago Press, 1980).

11. For a discussion of markets and hierarchies in alternative politico-economic systems, see Lindblom, *Politics and Markets.*

12. For the complex system of points and social distinctions employed for a time in Cuba, see Robert M. Bernardo, *The Theory of Moral Incentives in Cuba* (University, Ala.: University of Alabama Press, 1971), chapter 3. For arguments about the inevitability of inequality because of the division of labor and various social differentiations, see Lane, *The End of Inequality?*; Ralf Dahrendorf, "On the Origin of Social Inequality," in Laslett and Runciman, eds., *Philosophy, Politics and Society, Second Series,* pp. 88–109; and the debate between Melvin Tumin and Wilbert Moore in the *American Sociological Review* 28 (1963): 19–28. The latter concerns the extent to which a variety of separable inequalities must amount, in total, to a system of social stratification.

addition to the empirical evidence that it would be unrealistic to assume otherwise, there is a normative purpose served in applying this assumption. It has been characteristic of liberal—as distinct from radical—political theory to advocate equality of opportunities rather than equality of outcomes.[13] If we were to assume that strict equality of outcomes were achieved, then there would be little point in worrying about the fate of equal opportunity. Equal chances for equal outcomes would follow in an empty and formal sense from the mere fact of equal outcomes. As strict equality of outcomes is approached, the salience of equal opportunity as an issue can be expected to subside accordingly.

The argument that follows should be thought of as a test of the coherence and viability of this liberal focus on equal opportunity. Given the commitment of liberal theory to liberty, can its reliance on equal opportunity as an ultimate strategy of legitimation for distributional questions be maintained, even under ideal conditions? Hence, my focus will be on liberal theories that are committed to equal opportunity but not to equality of outcomes. Later I will explore the implications of relaxing this assumption.[14]

In the trilemma to be developed below, both principles of equal opportunity can be maintained only through severe sacrifice in the autonomy of families. But this argument will depend on the assumption just defined—that there are substantial social and economic inequalities in the society. If this assumption were relaxed, the conflict among our three principles would disappear. It is worth emphasizing the role of this assumption in the argument since it brings into focus a more general claim—that liberal theory, if taken seriously, must be

13. See n. 5, chapter 1. Also, see Lakoff, *Equality*, chapter 6; John Schaar, "Equality of Opportunity and Beyond," in J. Roland Pennock and John W. Chapman, eds., *Nomos IX, Equality* (New York: Atherton Press, 1967), pp. 228–50; and Michael Young's fantasy, *The Rise of the Meritocracy* (Harmondsworth, Eng.: Penguin Books, 1961).

14. See sections 4.4 and 5.1.

far more radical in its implications than has been imagined by its major proponents. For it would be difficult to imagine a defensible liberal ideal of equal opportunity that was not committed to *both* of the principles defined here (merit and equal life chances). Yet any such doctrine would require either a systematic sacrifice in the autonomy of the family or a systematic achievement of equal results (rather than merely opportunities) throughout the society. Either of these two latter options would be far more radical, and far less comfortable in its implications, than any doctrine of equal opportunity seriously advocated in liberal theory. It is worth adding that I hope to subject liberal theories to this kind of critical scrutiny, not because I think liberalism is bankrupt, but because I believe that any future, viable version of liberal theory must face up to certain hard choices.[15] The trilemma of conflicts arising for equal opportunity will provide a starting point for that kind of re-examination.

3.3 The First Option   Under the ground rules just specified, implementation of any two of these principles will render achievement of the remaining one virtually impossible. For example, the first and third principles rule out the second. The autonomy of the family protects parental efforts to influence the development of their children. Given background conditions of inequality, children from the higher strata will have been systematically subjected to differential developmental opportunities that can reliably be expected to advantage them in the process of meritocratic competition. Under these conditions, the principle of merit—applied to talents as they have developed under such unequal conditions—becomes a mechanism for generating unequal life chances.

It is just as if the continuing inequality of life chances in the

15. This examination can be viewed as a continuation of the one I began in *Tyranny and Legitimacy.* For a general characterization of liberalism see section 5.1 below.

warrior society example came about through parental influence on talent development. If the autonomy of the family protects the process whereby parents influence their children, and if the principle of merit is employed, no matter how scrupulously, to select the best warriors, these unequal conditions for talent development—when combined with equal consideration for talents as developed—produce unequal life chances. Children of the present warriors can be expected to win in the competition disproportionately.

Furthermore, if the relevant recent history involves conscientious efforts at strict compliance, then the principle of merit will itself tend to exacerbate these unequal conditions for talent development. For parents from the higher positions will be systematicaly distinguishable by their greater skill, their competence, and their familiarity with all the desirable characteristics that are taken to constitute "qualifications" in that society. When the process of talent development is protected by the autonomy of the family, advantaged parents can be expected to have systematically greater success inculcating these characteristics among their children.

Consider, in our society, all of the advantages that families from the higher strata can give to their children: private schools, culture in the home, a secure home environment, trips abroad, private lessons, an advantaged peer group, and successful role models. These are only the most obvious examples of differential developmental opportunities affecting both competence and motivation so as to give children from the higher strata systematic advantages in any system of meritocratic competition compatible with our second principle.[16]

Consider the overwhelming effect of family background on life chances that emerges from Jencks's study of the determinants of economic success among men in America:

16. See Jencks, *Inequality,* pp. 29–32, 76–81, 89–92, 135–246; Kenneth Keniston, *All Our Children: The American Family Under Pressure* (New York: Harcourt Brace Jovanovich, 1977), chapter 2; and Jencks, *Who Gets Ahead?,* chapters 3 and 12.

If we define "equal opportunity" as a situation in which sons born into different families have the same chances of success, our data show that America comes nowhere near achieving it. If, for example, an omniscient social scientist were to predict the economic standing of sons from different families he would find that sons from the most favored fifth of all families had predicted Duncan scores [a scale of occupational status running from 0 to 96] of about 64, while sons from the least favored fifth of all families have predicted scores of about 16.[17]

As Jencks notes, this is about the difference in status between a social worker and an auto mechanic. Or, if the outcomes are evaluated in terms of income,

the sons of the most advantaged fifth could expect to earn 150 to 186 percent of the national average, while the sons of the least advantaged fifth could expect to earn 56 to 67 percent of the national average.[18]

Of course, evidence from American society is only indirectly relevant to our problem of ideal theory since the other principle under discussion, the principle of merit, is only partially instituted in this society. Jencks, however, usefully identifies five basic causal mechanisms that generate unequal life chances in America; it is worth noting that all but one of them would be compatible with the fullest institutionalization of the principle of merit:

1. Men from advantaged backgrounds have cognitive skills that employers value.

2. Men from advantaged backgrounds have noncognitive traits that employers value.

3. Among men with similar cognitive and noncognitive

17. Jencks, Who Gets Ahead?, p. 82.
18. Ibid., p. 83.

traits, those from advantaged families have more educational credentials. Employers appear to value these credentials in their own right, even when they are not associated with measurable skills or behavior.

4. Among men with similar skills and credentials, those from advantaged families seek jobs in higher status occupations than those from disadvantaged families.

5. Even among men with similar skills and credentials who enter the same occupation, employers seem to pay men from advantaged families slightly more than men from disadvantaged families.[19]

The cognitive skills, noncognitive traits, and educational credentials referred to in mechanisms 1 to 3 can all count as qualifications compatible with our principle of merit.[20] Mechanism 4, the motivation to aspire to higher positions, is equally compatible with the principle. Only the fifth mechanism (unless it depends on factors of performance or motivation unmeasured in Jencks's data) might be interpreted as discrimination in terms of family background and, hence, as unacceptable in a society attempting to institute the principle of merit.

While empirical conditions will vary from one society to the next, the general proposition is difficult to deny: children from advantaged families in a given society will have greater opportunities to develop the skills, credentials, and motivations valued in that society. If the autonomy of the family protects the process by which parents provide those greater opportunities, and if the principle of merit sorts people accurately in terms of their skills, credentials, and motivations—as devel-

19. Ibid., pp. 70–71.

20. However, to the extent that credentials do not support the justificatory burden of predicting competence or motivation for performance in given positions, they should not be used as criteria, compatible with the principle of merit, for assignment to those positions. See Jencks, *Who Gets Ahead?*, p. 184, for a discussion of the overreward given the B.A. degree. Hence, some aspects of the operation of mechanism 3 in the quoted passage would not be compatible with the principle of merit.

oped under those unequal conditions—then systematic inequality of life chances will result.[21]

3.4 The Second Option   Suppose one were to keep the
autonomy of the family in
place but attempt, nevertheless, to equalize life chances? Institutionalizing the last two principles in this way would require
sacrifice of the first, the principle of merit. Given background
conditions of inequality, the differential developmental influences discussed in the last section produce disproportionate
talents and other qualifications among children in the higher
strata. If they must be assigned to positions so as to equalize
life chances, then they must be assigned regardless of these
differential claims. "Reverse discrimination" in favor of those
from disadvantaged backgrounds would have to be applied
systematically throughout the society.

By reverse discrimination, I mean any procedure of assignment that consistently places crucial weight on some characteristic other than qualifications (as defined earlier).[22] If qualifications have been appropriately defined, in a sense sufficiently
relevant to performance, then widespread assignment of those
who are less qualified can be expected to have a great cost in
efficiency.[23] It would also have a substantial cost in fairness.

21. The visibility given to extreme upward mobility should not obscure
such statistical propositions. As Harold Lasswell noted in his 1936 classic,
Politics: Who Gets What, When, How (New York: Meridian Books, 1958):
"Although any bright and talkative lad in the United States may be told that
one day he may be president, only eight boys made it in the last generation."
(p. 14). Lasswell then goes on to note the limited numbers of persons who
actually make it to other highly valued positions, despite the widely shared
character of the aspiration for those positions.
22. Such a procedure would discriminate against those who are more
qualified and in favor of those from disadvantaged backgrounds. For some of
the many contested uses of reverse discrimination see Barry R. Gross, *Discrimination in Reverse: Is Turnabout Fair Play?* (New York: New York University
Press, 1978), chapters 2 and 3. See also section 3.7 below.
23. See Daniels, "Merit and Meritocracy" and Goldman, *Justice and Reverse Discrimination*, chapter 2, for the efficiency goals served by merit. The
systematic sacrifice of merit considered here would sacrifice efficiency for

For the analogue of a competition in which skill and effort provide a sense in which people earn or merit their payoffs would no longer apply.[24]

Now the sacrifice in efficiency might be avoided if on-the-job training could make up entirely for deficiencies in earlier preparation. It is hard to believe, however, in a modern industrial society, with a complex differentiation of tasks, that qualifications that are performance-related could not be defined so as to predict better performances. Perhaps, in some actual societies, the definition of qualifications has not carried this justificatory burden. In those societies, apparently meritocratic competition has amounted to no more than an empty credentialism. That is just to say, the principle of merit has not actually been implemented in those cases,[25] for the principle required an appropriate competition in terms of qualifications—criteria that are job-related in that they fairly can be interpreted as indicators of competence or motivation for an individual's performance in a given position. To assign persons to positions regardless of qualifications in this sense is, by definition, to assign persons who are not as likely (as those more qualified) to perform well—insofar as that matter can be judged in terms of any prior indicators of talent or motivation as these might be displayed in a suitable competition. If there is a system of significant on-the-job training, then that must be taken into account in the prior definition of qualifications. Those who are most likely to profit or improve their performance from such training have to be given correspondingly

"arrays" of job assignments (as in Daniels's merit principle) or for individual job assignments (as in Goldman's formulation).

24. For the appeal of this model of a fair competition, embodied in the ideal of pure procedural justice, see Rawls, *Theory of Justice*, sections 12, 13, 14. It is worth noting that any institutionalization of such a fair competition can be expected to leave a substantial role for luck or chance. This is not worrisome so long as luck is not systematically maldistributed by class, race, or ethnic background.

25. For an inflated claim that this kind of credentialism has been the rule rather than the exception in apparently meritocratic assignment see George Gilder, *Wealth and Poverty* (New York: Basic Books, 1981), chapter 13.

greater consideration. Demonstration that one will be more educable on the job should itself be considered a kind of qualification.

I can think of one imaginary scenario that appears, at first glance, to evade this argument. Suppose there were a lottery system at birth that randomly assigned babies to families. The system of differential opportunities for talent development could be kept in place and the system of meritocratic assignment for talents, as developed under those conditions, could be fully instituted. The example is of interest because equal life chances, in a quite precise sense, would result from the arrangement. For the random system of assignment of newborn babies to families would serve to equalize life chances when judged from the perspective of newborns before the lottery. Any newborn infant's chance of reaching any highly valued position would be precisely equal to that of any other newborn infant. Should this admittedly bizarre and unpalatable arrangement be considered a relevant counterexample? Does it fulfill all three principles simultaneously?

The example does not overturn the argument, I believe, because it depends on a violation of the autonomy of families. The liberty of parents to raise their *own* children would have been interfered with coercively. The state would have forcibly determined which children are to be raised by which parents. By our initial principle, the liberty of parents to raise their own children can be interfered with only in order to ensure for children the essential prerequisites for adult participation in the society. While removal of a child from its parents might be justified then in some isolated cases of extreme deprivation (in order to shield the child from clearly harmful developmental conditions), such a wholesale process of reassignment clearly could not rest on such a basis. While some children might be benefited by the changes, others would be harmed.[26]

---

26. For a careful appraisal of the many risks in any reassignment of children to families see Goldstein et al., *Beyond the Best Interests of the Child*, part 2.

Perhaps some of this harm might be avoided through deception. Reassignment, however, even when coupled with deception in order to minimize experienced harm,[27] would still constitute coercive interference violating the autonomy of families. In defining family autonomy I assumed that natural parents have the initial option of *creating* families (subject to this principle) if they do so in a consensual manner, that is, one not subject to sustained and intense disagreement. This does not mean, of course, that parents may freely contribute to unrestrained population growth. For under some empirical conditions, such growth would endanger the prerequisites for childrens' future participation as adults in the society and, hence, may be coercively restricted in accordance with the autonomy principle.[28] Furthermore, this principle would even leave room for the state to intervene to prevent certain persons from procreating when it is clear that their offspring could not reasonably aspire to even the essential prerequisites for adult participation in the society (because of extreme disabilities or deformities). This principle would not require such government intervention, but it would place such procreation outside the sphere of action protected by the autonomy of families.[29]

In including within family autonomy the "initial option" of natural parents to create families, I explicitly identified the basis for rejecting the lottery system. The autonomy of families, if it is to be meaningful, must not only protect fully formed families, it must also protect the process by which they come into being. Wholesale reassignment of children to parents, or wholesale intrusion into the process by which parents consensually choose each other would violate the autonomy of

27. By experienced harm I mean harm within the subjective awareness of the persons involved. They may also be harmed, in the sense of their interests being sacrificed, without their ever knowing it. For a further critique of lottery proposals see section 4.2 below.

28. See Garrett Hardin, "The Tragedy of the Commons" and Michael D. Bayles, "Limits to a Right to Procreate," in Bayles, *Ethics and Population*.

29. I have in mind a case such as Tay-Sachs disease, where the harm to the possible child is both extreme and predictable.

families as much as would intrusion into established families.[30] Perhaps such a bizarre lottery scheme would realize equal life chances and the principle of merit. But like other systems that achieve these two principles, it would violate the remaining one, the autonomy of families.

There is a sense in which this scenario literally realizes the familiar metaphor of the "lottery" of birth. If that metaphor is taken seriously, one wonders how important it would be to actually undertake the random process of assignment to parents after birth. It is this latter process, of course, that violates the autonomy of families. But this metaphor of a "lottery of birth" depends on the relevance of an imaginary perspective from which we can coherently view ourselves as *potential* persons.[31]

Rawls's famous device of the "original position" depends, of course, on the coherence and viability of such an imaginary

30. I am indebted to James Billington for pointing out that the Soviet Union has used wholesale reassignment of children to suppress religious sects such as the Pentecostalists. The autonomy of the family defines an often unrecognized condition for the transmission of religious and ethnic pluralism from one generation to the next.

31. The potential persons interpretation creates anomalies for population policy. See R. M. Hare's critique of Rawls, based on the interests of potential persons in actually coming to exist, in "Rawls's Theory of Justice," Norman Daniels, ed., *Reading Rawls: Critical Studies of A Theory of Justice* (New York: Basic Books, 1975), pp. 31–107, especially pp. 97–101. Hare argues that if persons in the original position were not already sure of a place in society, their first interest would be to require procreation on a mass scale in order to maximize their chance of coming to be born. We might add that this anomaly could be avoided by an assumption that all members of the original position know that they are among the persons who happen to exist in the society. This strategy though would be subject to the problem that the continuation of the human race would not raise issues then that could be considered within the framework of the original position. If a given generation decided not to procreate, persons in the original position (choosing, out of self-interest, by hypothesis) would not have grounds for objection since they are to assume that they already have a place among the extant generations. Rawls has argued that individual interests continue over two generations, but this somewhat mysterious assumption has not been interpreted so as to produce a duty or requirement that one generation create the next. See Hare, "Rawls's Theory," p. 97, and Rawls, *Theory of Justice*, p. 128.

perspective. Yet, we can grant the relevance of a hypothetical construction of ourselves as potential persons (before we actually enter into existence) for certain theoretical purposes but not necessarily for others. When combined with certain other assumptions, it might offer a useful account of fairness for hypothetical choice (as in Rawls's original position), without also constituting the basis for a substantive principle of equal opportunity. The principle of equal life chances requires some actual, not hypothetical, benchmark from which our expectations are equalized. In this respect, it can be sharply distinguished from the original position.[32]

Accepting the hypothetical benchmark for the principle of equal life chances would trivialize the principle, for any society, no matter how stratified, oppressive, and inegalitarian, would embody equal life chances in this merely formal sense. If we can imagine ourselves reasoning about our life chances before we come into existence in a given society, there is a coherent sense in which we might think that our chances of being any given person are randomized.[33] Hence, my chances of being lord of the manor or a serf on a feudal estate could be thought of as the same as anyone else's from this perspective.[34] Such a feudal society could then be interpreted as equalizing life chances in this abstract, hypothetical sense. The principle interpreted this way would clearly have entirely different im-

32. See the discussion of the original position and other moral decision procedures in section 5.2. See also n. 34 below.

33. In the absence of further information, we can employ the principle of insufficient reason to treat the various possibilities as equally likely. As Rawls admits, there is then an argument that the expected value of our payoffs will be maximized by a society organized according to the principle of average utility. See Rawls, *Theory of Justice*, pp. 165–66.

34. Rawls offers the example of a slaveholder who cites gambling from the original position as a justification for a practice of slavery (conforming to the principle of average utility): "In the initial contractual situation he would choose the average principle even at the risk of its subsequently happening that he is justifiably held a slave" (p. 167). Rawls's claim is that the gambling argument is objectionable, although the hypothetical character of the agreement is not.

plications from the principle requiring equal life chances from a benchmark identifying actually existent persons. In this latter version, systematic implications follow for social mobility throughout the society. The core of its appeal would be sacrificed then by the alternative version.

Hence, a lottery among newborns, while it might succeed in equalizing life chances, would do so at the expense of the autonomy of the family and its connected private sphere of liberty—in particular, the liberty of parents to raise their own children. If the autonomy of families remains undisturbed, given background conditions of inequality, unequal developmental influences will produce a differential development of qualifications among those from the higher strata. These conditions force a hard choice between equality of life chances, on the one hand, and the principle of merit, on the other. The first option explored in the last section sacrificed the former. What I am calling the second option, outlined in this section, sacrifices the latter. Only a process of assignment that was applied regardless of meritocratic factors could equalize life chances despite differential talent development. Such a system of reverse discrimination,[35] systematically applied across the society, would appear inevitably to conflict with both efficiency and fairness.

We might imagine another hypothetical system that could conceivably ameliorate some of these conflicts. Suppose a nationwide lottery for job assignment were instituted not among newborns but among fully developed adults. The private sphere of liberty would remain in place with all of its effects on the unequal development of talents and other qualifications. Life chances would be equalized since the lottery

---

35. See n. 22 above and the discussion in the text. I am using the term "reverse discrimination" more broadly than some definitions that would restrict it to preferential treatment in favor of specified groups that had previously been discriminated against. For an example of this more restrictive definition, see the "working definition" in Barry Gross, ed., *Reverse Discrimination* (Buffalo, N.Y.: Prometheus Books, 1977), p. 3.

would strictly randomize the process of assignment to positions. Again, the principle sacrificed would be merit since
assignment would be accomplished entirely in disregard for
any qualification relevant to job performance.

Even though sacrificing meritocratic processes would di-
vorce the system of assignment from one kind of claim to
fairness, instituting the lottery would introduce another. Each
person would have an equal chance for any given position. No
one would have a special claim, based on any contingent
factors. Note that the principle of merit distinguished relevant
factors (qualifications) from irrelevant ones and based its claim
to fairness on insulating the system of assignment from influences by any of the irrelevant factors. In a sense, the job
assignment lottery would take this argument a step further by
simply considering all contingent factors—any basis for differentiating one adult from another—as irrelevant to the process
of job assignment. In doing so, it precludes applicants from
claiming, in any sense, that they have "earned" or "merited"
their positions through skill or effort. The model of a fair
competition, when supplanted by a lottery, treats all persons as
indistinguishable recipients of an equal chance.

Of course, it is likely that the sacrifice in efficiency would be
severe. Perhaps it might be ameliorated through systematic on-
the-job training. As noted before, however, in a modern society
with complex task differentiation, it seems undeniable that
there would be a substantial cost in efficiency. Even if primary
training were on the job, applicants could surely be differentiated in terms of their potential educability. If the private
sphere of liberty and background conditions of inequality were
maintained, then differential performance in a complex variety
of positions could be predicted. Therefore, compared to an
alternative system of merit, this system could be expected to
require a sacrifice in efficiency.

It might be objected that our presumption that parents will
differentially influence the talent development of their children rests, in part, on the expectation that those talents will be

of use in the later process of job assignment. If a society replaced meritocratic competition with a job lottery, perhaps this new institutional background would affect the motivation of parents to inculcate skills that eventually would be relevant to job performance. Since we are raising an empirical question about a hypothetical scenario, the answer is, to a large degree, indeterminate. Parents might be imagined to switch their focus to "well-roundedness," adaptability, and educability in unexpected circumstances, and other characteristics that might better serve their children in such a system. The essential point, however, is that regardless of the extent of the cost in efficiency, the principle of merit would have to be sacrificed by any such attempt to equalize life chances while maintaining the autonomy of families.

It is also worth noting that a job lottery alternative to merit would produce a conflict with liberty of a different kind. I defined the autonomy of families and the private sphere of liberty narrowly so as to clarify the role of the family in the trilemma of equal opportunity. Another kind of liberty, which falls outside the private sphere, is the liberty to seek and compete for employment. This liberty might be formulated in a strong way so that any interference with mutual consent between a potential employer and employee is unjustified. Even the principle of merit, in this view, might constitute unjustified coercion. Or the interests of competing potential applicants might be taken into account so that liberty to seek employment (and the corresponding liberty of employers to seek employees) might be constrained by requirements of fair competition like those specified by the principle of merit. This is a weak formulation of the liberty of employment.[36]

Liberty of employment, even in this quite weak sense, conflicts sharply with the job lottery proposal. While the proposal would leave the private sphere intact in an effort to

36. See the discussion of liberty of employment under perfect equality in section 4.4 below.

equalize life chances, it would produce conflicts with liberty in another recognizable and important sense, even when that liberty is defined modestly. If I want to be a pediatrician, yet my lottery ticket requires that I become a corporate lawyer, or if I want to be a violinist, yet my lottery ticket requires that I become an auto mechanic, my liberty of employment, indeed, my liberty to determine the basic direction of my life plan has been severely constrained.

Since my focus here has been on the private liberties involved in the family, I note this additional difficulty only in passing. Within the framework of our more general discussion, the point to note about this job lottery proposal is not its sacrifice of liberty of employment, but rather, its sacrifice of the principle of merit. Like all efforts to equalize life chances while maintaining the autonomy of families intact, it would sacrifice the third, remaining principle.

3.5 The Third Option   Suppose one were to attempt to equalize life chances while maintaining the system of meritocratic assignment. Given background conditions of inequality, it is the autonomy of families that protects the process by which advantaged families differentially affect the development of talents and other qualifications in their children. Only if this process were interfered with could both the principles of merit and of equal life chances be achieved. In other words, if equality of life chances is to be achieved through processes consistent with the principle of merit, then conditions for the development of talents and other qualifications must be equalized. Given background conditions of inequality, this can be done only through some mechanism that systematically insulates the development of each new generation from the unequal results achieved by the last. Coercive interferences with the family would be required if advantaged parents were to be prevented, systematically, from passing on cognitive, affective, cultural, and social advantages to their children. Perhaps a massive system of collectivized child-rearing could be devised to achieve such a result.[37] Anything short of such a large-scale alternative to the autonomous nuclear family would probably provide only an imperfect barrier between the inequalities of the parental generation and the developmental processes affecting its children.

From the communal child-rearing in Plato's *Republic* to the test tube nurseries in Huxley's *Brave New World*, the replacement of the family with some alternative strategy of child-rearing has been the centerpiece of any social engineering that required complete manipulation of human development.[38] As long as the private sphere of liberty is in place, crucial developmental factors are entrusted to the autonomous decisions of families and are, by that very fact, insulated from social control. Whether the efforts at social engineering are aimed at equalization or hierarchy, the family constitutes a crucial barrier to the manipulability of the causal factors affecting human development.

Whatever the precise institutional design, if developmental factors are to be equalized, systematic intrusion into the autonomy of families would be required. Recall that coercive interference into consensual family relations can be justified, according to the principles stated here, only to ensure the essential prerequisites for adult participation in the society— to assure a child's physical or mental health, his literacy, or his knowledge of the necessary social conventions. This principle defines a restrictive paternalistic burden that must be met if coercive interference is to be justified. This paternalistic bur-

37. For a mixed assessment of the comparatively small-scale Israeli experiment with various forms of collectivized child-rearing (among self-selected groups), see Bruno Bettelheim, *The Children of the Dream* (London: Thames and Hudson, 1969).

38. For an interesting argument that Plato's utopian proposals on the family and child-rearing were meant to be taken seriously, see Susan Moller Okin, *Women in Western Political Thought* (Princeton: Princeton University Press, 1979), part 1 and also the appendix to chapter 2 (for a critique of Bloom's views).

den is obviously not met by strategies that simply level down or equalize developmental influences in order to lessen the advantages of children in the upper strata. The interests of *those* children are not served at all by such efforts. And, provided that scarcity is not so extreme that such intrusions are necessary to ensure the essential prerequisites for children from other strata, it would have to be considered an intrusion into the autonomy of families. In other words, under the stated ground rules of ideal theory—for which we assumed only moderate scarcity—these leveling down strategies cannot be reconciled with the autonomy of families.

In the next section I will look into various strategies of intervention, by the government or other social institutions, that might "level up," rather than down, that might, in other words, increase the developmental opportunities of the lower strata, and still leave the autonomy of families intact. My general claim will be that such strategies of leveling up are either so paltry in their efficacy or so utopian in their expense that they cannot be expected to provide a solution to our problem.[39] While there is a compelling need to pursue them as far as possible, they cannot be expected to equalize developmental opportunities to the levels offered by more advantaged families. The only strategies of intervention that might offer a hope of the required massive effects would amount to such a wholesale change in the child's environment that their obviously prohibitive expense would violate any realistic construction of the budget constraint. Hence, leveling up strategies of intervention—that leave the private sphere intact—are either prohibitive in expense or insufficient in effect. On the other hand, by making many of the children affected worse-off (those who would have been advantaged without the equalization efforts), leveling down strategies clearly violate the autonomy of families if those provisions are to be universally enforced.

39. They are paltry when compared to the aspiration of full equalization. Many such programs, however much they fall short of the ideal, are urgently needed. See section 4.5 below.

They do not satisfy the restrictive, paternalistic burden required to justify such interventions.

3.6 Strategies of Intervention   The linchpin of the trilemma just outlined is the connection between the autonomy of families and the unequal development of talents and other qualifications that takes place under background conditions of inequality. If qualifications tend to develop unequally in this way, then we are faced with a hard choice between the principle of merit and equality of life chances. Those who have unequal opportunities to develop qualifications will have unequal life chances, if assignment to positions is governed by the principle of merit. Correspondingly, they can have equal life chances only if assignment to positions violates the principle of merit in a systematic manner. These two corners of the trilemma, the autonomy of the family and background inequalities, can be viewed as a dilemma of equal opportunity—a forced choice between two basic formulations of the concept.

It is worth pausing to explore further whether this crucial causal connection is unavoidable. Perhaps governments, or other organizations, might be able to intervene in a manner compatible with the autonomy of families, in order to equalize developmental opportunities, and thereby equalize life chances. Considerable evidence has recently accumulated that, while compensatory efforts can indeed improve the developmental opportunities facing the least advantaged, any realistic efforts will not be substantial enough to alter the basic pattern of conflict in the trilemma.

In the last section I alluded to two general strategies of intervention aimed at greater equality in the developmental influences on the formation of talents, motivations, and other qualifications. One strategy was called leveling up and the other, leveling down. The former achieves greater equality by improving the resources and opportunities available to the less advantaged strata, the latter achieves greater equality by lowering the resources and opportunities available to the more advantaged strata. If background conditions of inequality and a realistic budget constraint are both assumed, then the effects of both leveling up and leveling down strategies are predictable. Under these conditions, leveling up strategies must be insufficient to equalize developmental conditions. Leveling down strategies, on the other hand, must violate the autonomy of families. To be successful, they would have to intervene coercively to separate upper strata children from all of the advantages that their parents might attempt to give them.[40] Hence, the trilemma is not affected by such strategies since either the autonomy of the family must be sacrificed (by leveling down) or the inequality of developmental conditions basically is not affected. As we have seen, this inequality of developmental conditions requires, in turn, that we sacrifice either equality of life chances (if we institute the principle of merit) or the principle of merit (if we institute equality of life chances). Under any of the possible options, at least one of the three principles is sacrificed.

A great deal of recent research supports the view that schools, by themselves, must be insufficient to redress the developmental inequalities created by differing home environments. For example, one of the central conclusions arising from James Coleman's landmark study was:

> Altogether, the sources of inequality of educational opportunity appear to lie first in the home itself and the cultural influences immediately surrounding the home; then they lie in the school's ineffectiveness to free achievement from the impact of the home and in the school's cultural homogeneity which perpetuates the social influences of the home and its environs.[41]

40. Coercion would be necessary because universal compliance with such a disadvantageous solution could not be expected. See the discussion below.

41. James S. Coleman, "Equal Schools or Equal Students?," *The Public Interest* 4 (1966): 70–75. The quotation is from pages 73–74.

Coleman amplifies this conclusion in the report:

> One implication stands out above all: That schools bring little influence to bear on a child's achievement that is independent of his background and general social context; and that this very lack of an independent effect means that the inequalities imposed on children by their home, neighborhood, and peer environment are carried along to become the inequalities with which they confront adult life at the end of school.[42]

Of course, the mere fact that schools, as they now exist, have not equalized achievement across disparate home environments does not mean that some institutional innovations in the future might not provide for more perfect and more efficacious school systems. We cannot resolve questions of ideal theory merely by direct reference to the conclusions of empirical studies of actual institutions.

Yet such institutional innovations, if they were to affect our main conclusions, would have to take account of the freedom granted families, by the autonomy principle, to make decisions about *which* schools and other institutions their children will be subjected to. This freedom greatly restricts the manipulability of a crucial causal factor in the school environment—peer group influences.

The option of private schools is by itself a crucial barrier. It provides advantaged families an escape route from leveling down strategies of equalization. Such leveling down efforts could only be universally imposed on advantaged families at a cost in family autonomy. Families could not be expected to agree voluntarily and universally to an educational system designed explicitly to *disadvantage* their children (while comparatively advantaging children from less fortunate backgrounds). But unless participation in such a system were voluntary, it would violate the autonomy of families; unless it

42. Coleman, *Equality of Educational Opportunity*, p. 325.

were universal, it would fall short of equalizing developmental conditions across the society.[43]

As long as the autonomy principle is maintained, the basis for control over the crucial developmental influences—home environment, school, peer group, location—will rest within the family. Families sufficiently advantaged to exercise that control can be expected to opt out of any leveling down strategies of equalization, precisely because such strategies would otherwise disadvantage their children. By opting out they can ensure desirable peer groups for their own children in favorable educational environments; their decision, of course, will have an effect on the peer groups available to other children, those who have not been able, or who have not chosen, to opt out.

But suppose the option of opting out were universalized through a publicly supported voucher plan? Such proposals have many attractions. Yet, I believe, they cannot be expected to resolve the root problem I am focusing on here. First, they would not affect the crucial role of home environments, a factor to which I shall return in a moment. Second, a crucial characteristic of the schools one might imagine people opting into requires that *their* option of selectivity be maintained.

Because differential home environments will affect the academic resources and qualifications students bring with them to the selection process, upper strata children will maintain an advantage—even if a voucher plan were so munificent as to equal the tuition of the very best private schools (a possibility that raises serious questions for any realistic construction of the budget constraint). Furthermore, parents will vary greatly in their ability to select schools and schools will vary greatly in the criteria they use, in turn, to select students.

43. For one proposal that would sacrifice family autonomy by eliminating private schools and other parental investments in child development, see Bruce Ackerman's recent innovative book, *Social Justice in the Liberal State,* chapter 5. While Ackerman's proposal of an equal "liberal education" would require systematic efforts to counterbalance parental influences, there is no indication that it would yield equal life chances.

If, as advocates believe, a voucher plan is likely to improve the fit between the values and educational philosophies of parents and the school environments of their children, such an improvement, by itself, is unlikely to equalize developmental opportunities across sectors of society.[44] As Coleman points out in the citation above, the "cultural homogeneity" of public school environments (a by-product of districting and residential patterns) "perpetuates the social influences of the home and its environs." Voucher plans that protect the voluntary character of choice—both on the part of parents and on the part of schools—can be expected to produce even greater cultural homogeneity. Meanwhile, any efforts to eliminate this process of mutual choice so as to require exposure to equal developmental influences would clearly violate the autonomy principle.

Simply stated, only a mandatory routing of students to school environments, that was designed, systematically, to compensate for differential home environments, would affect the basic mechanism at work in our trilemma. According to such a plan, disadvantaged children would receive proportionately more resources and attention, while advantaged children would receive proportionately less, in order to equalize overall developmental conditions regardless of family background. Systematic leveling down, in other words, would be required. Such a routing of children to school environments could not realistically be expected of any voucher plan since parents who have exposed their children to more advantaged environments could not universally be expected (indeed, they would rarely be expected) to expose their children voluntarily to such system-

---

44. Thoughtful proponents, such as Coons and Sugarman in *Education by Choice*, argue on grounds of choice and liberty; their equality claims are carefully limited. They argue that a voucher plan will equalize the *availability* of choice, extending it to poor families; they do not argue that a voucher plan will equalize developmental conditions (p. 2). Furthermore, the voucher plan must be carefully designed if it is to avoid "economic class segregation." See their critique of the Friedman plan in chapter 11.

atic disadvantages. And if the exposure were not voluntary then it would violate the autonomy of families principle.

It may seem that in emphasizing the connection between the autonomy of families and the option of private schooling we are burdening an appealing principle with the weight of indefensible privilege. Yet in modern developed societies, the choice of which institutions outside the family a child will be subjected to is a crucial part of the influence families may exercise over their children. To the extent that parents (or families operating consensually) lose control over such choices, they have been supplanted by the state (or other institutions) as key paternalistic agents.[45] Perhaps ultimately this kind of change would be justified in the interests of equalizing developmental opportunities. Its impact, however, on the autonomy of families should not be underestimated.

Thus far, the policies mentioned would affect choice of schooling either by closing it off through forced attendance at certain schools or by widening it through the use of voucher plans. I have not yet considered preschool efforts aimed at ameliorating disadvantages in home environments.

Urie Bronfenbrenner, in a systematic review of research on early childhood interventions, concludes that the crucial developmental factor in their success or failure is their effect on what he calls the "mother-child dyad as an interactive system."[46] This dyad (or a comparable one between a child and some other relatively permanent adult such as a father or a surrogate parent) is a crucial component in the child's cognitive and emotional development:

45. For a history of institutional encroachments upon the family; see Christopher Lasch, *Haven in a Heartless World: The Family Besieged* (New York: Basic Books, 1977).

46. U.S., Department of Health, Education and Welfare, *A Report on Longitudinal Evaluations of Preschool Programs: Is Early Intervention Effective?* vol. 2, by Urie Bronfenbrenner (Washington, D.C.: Office of Child Development, 1974), p. 26.

Any force or circumstance which interferes with the formation, maintenance, status or continuing development of the parent-child system in turn jeopardizes the development of the child.[47]

Strategies of intervention intended to improve the developmental opportunities of the less advantaged might usefully be divided into:

a. those that do not attempt to affect this mother-child system but rather attempt to *supplement* it by offering the child other developmental opportunities;

b. those that do attempt to affect this mother-child system by *strengthening* it; and

c. those that attempt to *replace* it with some alternative compatible with the child's existing family assignment.

Generally, early preschool education in a group setting falls into the first category. Certain efforts at intervention in the home environment fall into the second. And "ecological interventions" that provide the child a virtually new environment fall into the third.

One difficulty with preschool interventions in a group setting is that substantial gains, at least in IQ, have not been made beyond the first years of intervention, no matter how long the program is continued. Furthermore, the results have been transient:

In general, one year after intervention is terminated, the IQ of the "graduates" begins to drop, the difference between the experimental and control groups gradually decreases, the once impressive gains are reduced to a few points, and, what is most crucial, the average IQ of the experimental group often falls back into the problem range of the lower 90s and below.[48]

47. Ibid., p. 31.
48. Ibid., p. 14.

Since Bronfenbrenner rendered these pessimistic conclusions in 1975, a new wave of somewhat more optimistic findings has emerged. Some long-term effects on scholastic achievement (as contrasted to IQ) do seem to result from early participation in programs such as Head Start. As the preface to the most enthusiastic volume of new findings notes, however:

> Early intervention does not assure that the children will perform as well as the average child in the population. The benefits of early intervention over non-intervention are striking, but comparison of the children in early intervention programs with grade norms for 4th, 5th and 6th grades is not impressive. The children are behind the average child in the population.[49]

Compared to control groups of children from similar backgrounds, children from early intervention programs do show some long-term scholastic gains. But these gains are largely a matter of the *prevention of loss* that would otherwise have occurred. Children from these programs fall behind less rapidly than control groups from similar backgrounds, though they still fall behind the norms for their grade levels.

Furthermore, the most striking positive effects have been on the assignment of children to special education classes (for the learning disabled) and on retention in grade. Compared to control groups, early intervention children are far less likely to be held back and are less likely to be assigned to special remedial classes. While these are important improvements, they are far short of the effects that would be required were early intervention to equalize developmental conditions regardless of family background.

Home-based programs directed explicitly at affecting patterns of parent-child interaction have achieved more lasting gains in IQ than have preschool programs in a group setting.

49. Bernard Brown, ed., *Found: Long-Term Gains From Early Intervention* (Boulder, Co.: Westview Press, 1978); the quotation is from the Preface by Edith H. Brotberg, p. xviii.

Yet, these home-based programs are also notable for what might be called the "climbing control group" (untreated subjects who also improve notably). These studies involved an "admission requirement that parents be interested and willing to enroll their child in the program even at the risk he might end up in the control group."[50] As Bronfenbrenner concludes:

> The climbing control group resulted from the self-selection of families in terms of their motivation to provide educational experience for the child. The more motivation was required, the more selective the sample of parents, and the more likely their children were to make a gain in IQ even if not admitted to the intervention program.[51]

There is no doubt that home-based strategies of intervention aimed at strengthening patterns of parent-child interaction have been comparatively successful in producing more lasting gains in IQ. Yet, the resultant gains are also subject to erosion and have not been reflected in school performance measures, for example, reading programs.[52] Furthermore, they depend crucially on the self-selection of parents in terms of motivation. The generalizability of their results in any large-scale application throughout the society is, therefore, extremely dubious. So this approach, while helpful, should not be viewed as a solution to our basic problem since it is only applicable to families in which parents are especially motivated.

The most impressive gains in IQ have been achieved by massive ecological interventions, those that replace a child's home environment with a new one. For example, a Milwaukee project matched twenty newborn children from deprived backgrounds with twenty paraprofessionals who acted as mother replacements for each child throughout the working day. Meanwhile, the children's mothers underwent training relevant to both child-rearing and employment. In each case, both

50. Bronfenbrenner, *Early Intervention* p. 21.
51. Ibid.
52. Ibid., p. 37.

mother and child were exposed to a carefully sequenced phase
of educational activities. By the age of five and a half the
children showed impressive gains in IQ compared to a control
group.[53] Instead of the eight to thirteen points in IQ gained
from the most successful group interventions, or the fourteen
to sixteen points in IQ gained by the most successful parent
intervention programs, ecological intervention programs like
this one achieved gains of over twenty-five points.[54]

Two caveats should be noted immediately about this strategy: First, "the program is, and will continue to be, as expen-
sive as it is effective, perhaps more so. And in terms of large-
scale applicability, the costs are prohibitive."[55] Second, the
long-term psychological effects of the program are unknown.
The improvement in children's cognitive development may
have to be balanced against harmful effects:

> Whatever happens to them intellectually, serious ques-
> tions arise about their development in other spheres, espe-
> cially in terms of identity formation in their relation to
> their family or to other children in the neighborhood from
> whom they are partially isolated so long as they continue
> in the program.[56]

Given the potential for harm to the child, such a strategy of
radical separation and virtual replacement of the parent could
be justified—in a manner compatible with the autonomy of
families—only in cases where the alternative of leaving the
child in the care of its parents clearly involved severe harm,

53. Ibid., p. 45. See also Rick Heber, Richard Dever, and Julianne Conry,
"The Influence of Environmental and Genetic Variables on Intellectual Development," in Herbert J. Prehm, Leo A. Hamerlynck, and James E. Croson, eds.,
Behavioral Research in Mental Retardation (Eugene, Oregon: University of
Oregon, Rehabilitation Research and Training Center in Mental Retardation,
monograph no. 1, 1968) pp. 1–22, especially pp. 19–21. For some methodological criticisms see Ellis B. Page, "Miracle in Milwaukee: Raising the IQ,"
Educational Researcher 1, No. 10 (October 1972): 8–16.
54. Bronfenbrenner, *Early Intervention*, p. 49.
55. Ibid., p. 46.
56. Ibid.

endangering some of the essential prerequisites discussed earlier. Hence, the applicability of this strategy would have to be limited to those in the severest circumstances, even if its expense could be supported. The expense, we might add, of full-time care on a one-to-one basis would be prohibitive, at the large-scale, by any plausible construction of our realistic budget constraint.

Setting aside the question of expense, any large-scale application of this strategy would presumably violate the autonomy of families. Parents—even those who are relatively disadvantaged in the judgment of social policy makers—could not be expected to relinquish, universally and voluntarily, their children to virtually full-time care by paraprofessionals. They would retain their parental role then in name only. Even when others might judge the children to be marginally better-off, this judgment is inevitably controversial and the parents cannot be expected, except in extreme and unusual cases, to agree. Furthermore, practical experience in this field supports the conclusion that disruption of intact families usually does more harm than good to the child, except in the most extreme cases of deprivation or abuse.[57] Hence this last strategy, which really amounts to parent replacement by paraprofessionals, cannot be considered a solution that avoids our trilemma since it requires sacrifice of one of the three essential principles, the autonomy of families.

In other words, even if the realistic budget constraint were set aside, it is safe to assume that no system of wholesale replacement of parents with paraprofessionals would be entered into voluntarily on a universal basis by all those whose children it would benefit. Yet coercive intervention, compatible with the autonomy of families, could be justified only where lack of essential prerequisites for the children was in question. Otherwise, if parents chose to take primary responsibility for child-care themselves, they could be prevented from

57. See Goldstein et al., *Beyond the Best Interests*, pp. 3–8, 48–52.

doing so only at the cost of sacrificing one of our three principles. Given the centrality of parental roles in most of our
lives, this result is only to be expected. One might object that,
if indeed the children would be benefited, parents in those
cases should be forcibly supplanted from most of their influence. Yet, I believe that the autonomy of families assumption,
as I have defined it here, accurately captures the extent of
protection from such social policies that we would customarily give to the family. Parents deserve protection from social
interference (given that they satisfy certain essential prerequisites for their children) even when others might judge that
their children could be raised better by someone else.

In summary, while both group and home-based programs
produce some significant gains, even in the long-term, they fall
far short of equalizing developmental conditions throughout
the society regardless of class background. The massive ecological intervention exemplified by the Milwaukee experiment
might so transform the total environment of the child as to
approach equalization of developmental conditions. It could
not be adopted universally, however, without violating the
autonomy of families (and any plausible construction of a
realistic budget constraint as well). It seems reasonable to
conclude, therefore, that the recent wave of institutional experimentation with early childhood intervention does not offer
any results that would affect the basic trilemma of relations
outlined earlier. While those experiments suggest many ave-
nues for social policies that are urgently needed, they all fall far
short of equalizing developmental influences, regardless of
family background, through a strategy of intervention that
would be feasible as a large-scale solution.

The general problem is that leveling up strategies compatible with the autonomy of families can expose children to new
developmental influences only with the voluntary cooperation
of their families (given the caveats noted earlier in the autonomy principle). The more far-reaching the developmental influences required, the closer the intervention would approach

the parent-supplanting example of the Milwaukee experiment cited above. Complete manipulability of causal factors could be achieved only by something approaching replacement of the parents altogether, and it cannot be expected that this sort of extreme dislocation of intact families would be entered into voluntarily by all of those whose children would be benefited. On the other hand, forced participation would violate the autonomy principle. And nonuniversal participation would fail to resolve the problem since it would fail to equalize developmental conditions throughout the society.

An alternative strategy of intervention aimed at some direct effect upon the character of parent-child interaction in the home has already been mentioned. If parents are not to be replaced, they may be transformed. This strategy's success depends heavily on the willingness and ability of parents to cooperate. For this reason experiments involving self-selected parents, who are especially motivated, cannot be generalized to the population at-large.[58] Home-based strategies confront the problem noted above; if the modification of developmental influences is to be substantial enough to approach equalization, universal participation (at least among all those whose children might be thought to benefit) cannot be expected to come about voluntarily. In so intimate and salient an area of private liberty as parent-child relations, any transformation of behavior on a mass scale is bound to encounter opposition. The coercion, however, that would be required to bring about universal compliance would violate the autonomy principle. On the other hand, selective rather than universal participation would fail to achieve equalization of developmental conditions throughout the society.

The autonomy of families principle therefore provides a significant impediment to leveling up strategies just as it does

58. See Bronfenbrenner, *Early Intervention*, pp. 35-38. For more on the home-based strategy see P. Levenstein, "Cognitive Growth in Preschoolers through Verbal Intervention with Mothers," *American Journal of Orthopsychiatry* 40 (1970): 426–32.

to leveling down strategies. Except when certain essential prerequisites are at stake, it would prevent the state from manipulating developmental conditions without family consent. Systematic leveling down strategies, if made universal, would clearly violate the autonomy principle. It would be hopelessly unrealistic to expect advantaged parents to consent voluntarily and universally to conditions that were explicitly designed to render their children worse off.[59] But any effective leveling down strategy would, by definition, have that result. Conversely, leveling up strategies are either insufficient to close the gap in developmental conditions across different family backgrounds, or they must violate the autonomy of families in order to achieve, universally, a full manipulation of the required developmental conditions, either through replacement or through transformation of conditions within the family.

Suppose, however, that all potential parents were subjected to systematic indoctrination, or thought control, so that by the time they reached procreation they could universally be expected to comply "voluntarily" with systematic government intervention into their child-rearing practices. Or they would systematically conform without any further government intervention to whatever behavior was required and, if they believed themselves unable to conform, they would refrain from having children. A hypothetical reform like this might appear to remedy all the disadvantages now suffered by some children because their parents lack motivation or competence, or have a distinctive conception of appropriate child-rearing practices that places their children at a disadvantage. While economic irregularities would remain, there is no doubt that many developmental disadvantages might be overcome by such a reform. Would it escape the objection, however, that it violates the autonomy principle?

59. See note 1 of this chapter for the limits of the strict compliance assumption.

To answer this question, I must return to the definition of "coercive interferences" in the autonomy principle.[60] If universal and apparently voluntary compliance were to come about through a campaign of indoctrination that suppressed certain alternatives and promoted others, it would count as coercive interference and would violate the autonomy principle. According to the earlier definition, if knowledge of the alternatives to action A has been suppressed,[61] a person has been coerced into doing A just as effectively as if he had been threatened with dire consequences for performing any of those alternatives. Suppression and thought control may be as effective as punishment. The autonomy principle could be trivialized unless it also provided protection against such efforts at manipulating a person's awareness and understanding of alternatives.

It might be objected also that I have rested the analysis of this section too heavily upon recent American experience. Perhaps other strategies of intervention would be more effective than those that have been tried recently in this country. Furthermore, there is certainly no reason to focus meritocratic criteria for assignment on IQ. After all, our definition of qualifications was quite general and efforts to boost IQ (an admittedly controversial measure)[62] should be considered only a particular case of a more general problem.

In response, it is worth emphasizing that I invoked recent American experience for illustrative purposes only. The examples cited serve to reveal the general impediment posed by the

---

60. See section 2.4 above.

61. Suppression in this definition presumes intentionality. And it applies with respect to *known* alternatives and our evaluation of them. One should not expect to consider synoptically all of the possible alternatives. See David Braybrooke and Charles E. Lindblom, *A Strategy of Decision: Policy Evaluation as a Social Process* (New York: The Free Press, 1963), part 1.

62. For a systematic review see Block and Dworkin, *The IQ Controversy*, part 4. For a discussion of operational criteria for test fairness see Robert L. Linn, "Fair Test Use in Selection," *Review of Educational Research* 43 (1973): 139–61.

autonomy of the family principle to any systematic efforts to equalize developmental conditions regardless of family background. Some leveling up efforts will undoubtedly accomplish a great deal. There is no reason to believe, however, that any strategy might be devised that would leave the autonomy of families in place and, at the same time, equalize developmental conditions across families from different socioeconomic strata. Leveling down strategies can expect to encounter resistance from advantaged families because, whatever the precise form, such strategies are designed to render children worse off. On the other hand, leveling up strategies, whatever the precise form, must be insufficient to close the gap unless they involve a complete manipulation of all the significant causal factors affecting the disadvantaged child. Such a manipulation could be accomplished, I have speculated, either through wholesale supplanting of the parental role, as in the Milwaukee experiment, or through some complete transformation of parent-child patterns of interaction. Whatever the precise mechanism of intervention, *universal* compliance with such a radical change in so intimate and central an area of private liberty as parent-child relations could only be expected were coercion to be employed. Hence the impediment posed to strategies of intervention by the autonomy principle.

3.7 Preferential Treatment and Compensation for the Past

My central argument for the trilemma of equal opportunity presumes the conditions of ideal theory. Realization of any two of our principles reasonably can be expected to preclude the third under the ideal conditions of both strict compliance (in the present and relevant recent past) and only moderate scarcity. No reference to any legacy of injustice is necessary to produce a forced choice among the three stated principles. In this sense, simultaneous commitment to all three of our principles, given background conditions of inequality, produces an incoherent ideal for public policy, even under favorable conditions.[63]

If a coherent and defensible position is to be reached, this pattern of conflict requires some modification of our usual commitment to all three principles. One strategy would explicitly establish priority relations justifying the required sacrifice in one of the three principles. Another strategy would require abandoning one or more of the principles entirely and, perhaps, replacing others with a quite different principle. A third strategy would modify the character of our commitment to these principles, rather than the character of the principles themselves. If we regard them only as prima facie principles, to be traded off intuitionistically, one against another, in each particular case of conflict, then we have arrived at a defensible if limited kind of non-theory. While such a nonsolution to the problem of equal opportunity would be dissatisfying to many, it would avoid the difficulties raised by any commitment to fulfill *simultaneously* all three principles.[64]

I will later return to these various strategies available for ideal theory. For the moment, however, it may be useful to place this theoretical discussion in the context of recent American policy. What does this analysis suggest about recent efforts in the United States to provide preferential treatment according to native characteristics such as race, sex, or ethnic origin, motivated in part to compensate for a legacy of past discrimination? To what extent are these policies compatible with the liberal framework of individualistic competition em-

63. It would be incoherent as a guide to possible social choices when this empirical analysis is accepted and when our commitments to these principles are strong rather than weak or prima facie. See n. 12, chapter 2 above.

64. See section 5.2 below. For a general discussion of responses to conflict among ethical criteria see Brian Barry and Douglas Rae, "Political Evaluation," section 2, in Fred I. Greenstein and Nelson W. Polsby, eds., *Handbook of Political Science*, 9 vols. (Reading, Mass.: Addison-Wesley, 1975), 1: 337–401.

ployed here? How does the departure from ideal theory, because of our actual history of discrimination against various groups, affect the analysis?

Starting from the basic liberal notion of a fair competition among individuals for unequal positions in society, two principles explicitly concerned with equal opportunity were reached—merit and equality of life chances. It would be surprising and disturbing were any recognizably liberal theory forced to relinquish its commitment to either of these. Given background conditions of inequality, however, we are forced to choose between realization of both these principles and the autonomy of the family. As indicated earlier, the latter principle identifies the core area of negative liberty that is most central to the way most of us have structured our lives. It would be equally disturbing and surprising were any liberal theory forced to relinquish its commitment to realizing this principle, even under ideal conditions.

This trilemma of forced choice under ideal conditions suggests a minimum requirement for acceptable public policies, even under less than ideal conditions. It seems reasonable to require that no sacrifice in one of these three central principles should be undertaken *unless the sacrifice is necessary for a gain in one or more of the other two*, or unless there is some other valuable gain (according to other principles that would then have to be argued for, in turn). It is one thing to sacrifice a principle when the sacrifice is absolutely necessary to realize one or more other precious goals. It is quite another thing to sacrifice it when there is not such a corresponding gain (or even a prevention of loss) in some other important value.

This minimum condition seems extremely weak, since it prescribes nothing for the enormous range of cases where we must choose between sacrificing one or more of these values and preserving or improving the realization of one or more others. Despite this obvious incompleteness, this minimum condition does support a clear line of argument against certain practices of preferential treatment that are actually employed in the present American policy context. Some of the practices that proved most controversial in the recent debates over the *DeFunis* and *Bakke* cases would, in fact, fail this minimum condition.[65]

Before turning to such cases of reverse discrimination, I will distinguish them from several weaker varieties of preferential treatment. It is worth emphasizing that many practices labeled "affirmative action" do not even imply preferential treatment for minority group members in the actual process of assignment. By forcing institutions to report certain kinds of information, they are meant only as procedural safeguards for ensuring nondiscrimination. A similar point can be made about requirements that positions not be filled through "word-of-mouth contact"[66] or through systems that grant preference to relatives of current employees (a practice once common among unions and employers in the construction trades in the United States).[67] Other requirements ensure procedural fairness through an extremely weak kind of preferential treatment in the solicitation and recruitment of applicants. Special efforts to encourage a wider and more diverse pool of applicants can increase access to the competitive process for groups that might not be represented otherwise. Whether preferential treatment in any stronger sense is involved would depend on how those applicants are evaluated later in the assignment process, compared to applicants who are not from the designated special groups.

Other practices of apparent preferential treatment may really amount to no more than guarantees of procedural fair-

65. See the arguments below in this section against preferential treatment merely on grounds of race and in favor of preferential treatment when it is directed at the disadvantaged. Strangely enough, while the program the Supreme Court refused to rule on in *DeFunis* would fail the minimum condition proposed here, the program the court struck down in *Bakke* would pass it.

66. U.S. Commission on Civil Rights, *Statement on Affirmative Action*, Clearinghouse Publication 54 (Washington, D.C.: U.S. Government Printing Office, 1977), p. 3.

67. Ibid.

ness when they involve special care in the interpretation of data from persons who come from disadvantaged backgrounds or from differing cultural milieu. Some standardized tests may fail to measure accurately an applicant's real competence; apparent differential treatment may really amount in such cases to no more than conscientious efforts to make up for biases in the instruments of evaluation. I will set aside such measurement problems here since efforts to overcome them do not truly constitute cases of preferential treatment. Such efforts are, of course, entirely compatible with the principle of merit. In fact, they would be required by it.

It is also worth mentioning some very weak forms of preference that might be given in the actual assignment process. A ceteris paribus preference to break ties is sometimes employed. Members of a specified group are chosen, in other words, provided they are equally qualified. This kind of preferential practice does not involve a serious sacrifice of merit since, by definition, those chosen must be equally qualified. Nevertheless, it is worth noting that such practices are far from trivial in their implications, since they may substantially affect the probability that members of other (nonminority) groups will be chosen. Instead of an equal chance in cases of ties, nonminority group members must lose out in such cases. They must, in other words, do better than equally well in the competitive process in order to gain a position. To see that such a weak form of ceteris paribus preference is nontrivial, consider our reaction to it when it is practiced against rather than in favor of a given minority group. If an employer consistently refused to hire equally qualified blacks this would constitute objectionable descrimination—even if he were willing to hire blacks when they were more qualified than their competitors. Even when discrimination against a minority group takes this weak form, we still rightly consider it discrimination. Instead of equal consideration, in the sense of an equal chance for those with equal qualifications, members of the designated group must do better when they are discriminated against in this way. A ceteris paribus preference, in other words, is a denial of equal consideration of one's qualifications and should be considered more than a trivial departure from the principle of merit, even though those chosen must be equally qualified.

The kind of preferential treatment now often practiced is far more potent than this weak, ceteris paribus variety. Let us say that a practice of preferential treatment amounts to "reverse discrimination" if it produces significant and widespread sacrifice of the principle of merit in assignment in order to favor some specified group defined in terms of arbitrary native characteristics (such as race, sex, or family background).[68] By a significant sacrifice in the principle of merit in any given case, I mean simply the choice of those who are substantially less qualified over those who are more qualified, as those qualifications would be impartially assessed for the position in question.

Such reverse discrimination was, of course, the issue in the *DeFunis* and *Bakke* cases where preferential treatment went beyond the various weak measures cited above. It went beyond ensuring nondiscrimination, an appropriately broad applicant pool, and an accurate assessment of qualifications despite possible biases in the instruments of measurement. Preferential treatment in these cases clearly involved a substantial sacrifice in merit considerations as they might be applied regardless of race, sex, or other arbitrary native characteristics.

For example, in the *DeFunis* case all but one of the minority students admitted to the University of Washington Law School ahead of DeFunis rated lower on the university's "predicted first year average," a composite of grades and the law school admissions test that provided the primary basis for evaluating applicants. Furthermore, thirty of the minority students had scores so low that "but for their racial classification [they] would have been *summarily rejected*" (emphasis added).[69] And considering all indicators of qualifications, in addition to

68. Reverse discrimination is thus preferential treatment that is both systematic and widespread.

69. Brief of the Anti-Defamation League of B'nai B'rith as amicus curiae, *DeFunis.* p. 9. See also Sindler, *Bakke, DeFunis, and Minority Admissions.*

grades and test scores, the university admitted the sacrifice in meritocratic criteria resulting from this process but contended, nevertheless, that it was justified by the greater racial diversity that resulted.[70]

Preferential treatment in this case fit a pattern that is now quite common in highly competitive meritocratic contexts. Even though some of the arguments for the program made reference to economic, social, and cultural disadvantages, preferential treatment was instituted merely on the basis of racial classifications. As Bickel and Kurland pointed out in their amicus curiae brief:

> There is no pretense in this record that the assumption of cultural and economic disadvantage as applied to any particular individual applicant rested on anything but his race, or that the contrary assumption, namely, that an applicant had the normal cultural and economic advantages, in turn, rested on anything but the applicant's race. . . . And the evidence is clear that no effort was made to examine the mass of applications for individuals of cultural or economic deprivation, whatever the race of the applicant.[71]

Although socioeconomic disadvantages purportedly provided a justification for preferential admissions, the actual practice adopted separated applicants merely by race or ethnic origin. Marian Wright Edelman in another amicus curiae brief argued that these classifications were entirely appropriate:

> For it was the racial minorities generally—not just their "disadvantaged" or "poor" or "culturally deprived" members—that had suffered in the past from pervasive racial discrimination and *de facto* exclusion from law school and

Sindler concludes: "In short, had these 30 minority admittees been white, they would have been turned down summarily." (pp. 37-38).

70. Testimony from the Dean of the Law School is cited by Bickel and Kurland in Brief of the Anti-Defamation League of B'nai B'rith as amicus curiae, pp. 9-10.

71. Ibid., pp. 12–13.

the legal profession, which were the problems the School sought to remedy. In that sense, *all members of the minority groups were relevantly "disadvantaged" for the purposes of the University policy.*[72]

If this practice of preferential treatment *merely* according to race were to be defended, it would require a sharp departure from the liberal framework I have been employing here. For the significant sacrifice in the principle of merit was not counterbalanced by any gain in the other two principles I have been employing—equality of life chances or the autonomy of the family. In this sense it stands in stark contrast to another kind of preferential treatment program, one designed to help only those who had themselves suffered developmental disadvantages. If preferential treatment were awarded according to developmental disadvantages that had actually been suffered, as these might be roughly ascertained by income and class, or even by more specific information, then the cost in merit might arguably be counterbalanced by an improvement in equality of life chances. Persons who might otherwise never have a realistic chance of attaining certain positions because of unequal developmental opportunities, would see their chances improved by such a system.[73]

Such a program would be entirely compatible with the basic liberal framework of individualistic competition analyzed here. It would be designed to redress the inequality in developmental opportunities that, arguably, renders the competitive process objectionable because of its lack of background fairness. It would make up for the fact that in the first place some people never really would have had a chance to develop the skills and qualifications demanded by meritocratic competition.

This improvement in background fairness stands in sharp

72. Brief for the National Council of Jewish Women and others as amici curiae, *DeFunis*, p. 59.

73. For a similar proposal see Goldman, *Justice and Reverse Discrimination*, pp. 194–95.

contrast to the effects of a program of preferential treatment for racial or ethnic groups *as such*. Even proponents of such programs admit that many of the beneficiaries will be persons who are not disadvantaged themselves. As the University of California at Davis acknowledged in its Bakke brief, only about one third of the underrepresented minorities accepted in our nation's medical schools in 1976 had parental incomes under $10,000.[74] There was also considerable speculation whether DeFunis, a Sephardic Jew from a relatively poor background who had to work his way through college and law school, might reasonably have been considered more disadvantaged than many of the middle-class minority students admitted ahead of him.[75]

Terence Sandalow, an advocate of preferential treatment identifies the general issue:

> It is reasonable to suppose that a substantial percentage of the (not otherwise admissable) minority applicants who have the best chance of success in law school and the professions come from backgrounds that cannot plausibly be considered disadvantaged. Opponents of minority preferences have found it especially galling that the child of a wealthy and well-educated professional should receive preferential treatment simply because of his or her race.[76]

74. Brief for Petitioner, The Regents of the University of California v. Allan Bakke, p. 37, n. 46. This point is also made in the Brief of the American Jewish Committee and others as amici curiae, *Bakke*, p. 37, n. 18. Of course, I do not mean to imply that all of these students were admitted as a result of preferential treatment.

75. See the Washington Supreme Court opinion, DeFunis v. Odegaard, 82 Wn.2d 11, 507 p.2d 1169 (1973), C. J. Hale (dissenting), reprinted in Robert M. O'Neil, *Discriminating Against Discrimination* (Bloomington: Indiana University Press, 1975), p. 203–05. See also Michael J. Malbin, "The Court Ought to Decide for Mr. DeFunis" *The New York Times*, 12 April 1974, p. 31. On DeFunis's financial situation see Sindler, *Bakke, DeFunis, and Minority Admissions*, pp. 38–39.

76. Terence Sandalow, "Racial Preferences in Higher Education: Political Responsibility and the Judicial Role," *University of Chicago Law Review* 42 (Summer 1975): 691.

Despite this difficulty, Sandalow would oppose reshaping special admissions programs "to focus upon disadvantaged applicants" because this "would also force the exclusion of some of the ablest minority applicants."[77]

Kent Greenawalt, another advocate of preferential treatment by race, acknowledges the same problem, which he calls a serious problem of "overinclusiveness."[78] He offers, however, a novel argument for preferring such minority group members, even if they are not from disadvantaged backgrounds:

> If one effect of discrimination is that fewer blacks can qualify without preference, then one proper form of compensation is to eliminate the effect of denial of admissions on those who would otherwise have qualified. The closest a law school may be able to come to identifying the class of those who in the absence of discrimination probably would have qualified without preference is to choose the best prepared blacks who now apply.[79]

There are several complexities in this counterfactional claim that I shall discuss below. For the moment, it is worth noting that if one were to attempt consistently to imagine a version of American society in which previous discrimination toward blacks had never occurred, there is little reason to believe that those particular blacks who now are in a position to benefit from preferential treatment (merely according to racial characteristics) are "those who would otherwise have qualified" if there had been no legacy of injustice against blacks. Surely the compensatory claim is far stronger for present members of the ghetto underclass. Who knows where they would be now but for the "lengthening shadow of slavery" and its effect on their family structure and the social prison of poverty.[80] There is no

77. Ibid.
78. Kent Greenawalt, "Judicial Scrutiny of 'Benign' Racial Preference in Law School Admissions," in Gross, ed., *Reverse Discrimination*, p. 222.
79. Ibid., p. 224.
80. See John E. Fleming et al., *The Lengthening Shadow of Slavery: A Historical Justification for Affirmative Action for Blacks in Higher Education* (Washington, D.C.: Howard University Press, 1976).

reason to believe that those blacks who are presently "best prepared" offer even a remote approximation to those blacks "who in the absence of discriminations probably *would have* qualified" (emphasis added). I will explore in some detail some of the more surprising implications of taking these counterfactuals seriously. In the meantime, it is worth noting that this strategy for dealing with the overinclusiveness problem is open to serious objections.

The main point is that given the differential developmental effects upon more advantaged minority group members—advantages resulting from the income, family stability, peer groups, and schooling that their parents can make available to them—it is only reasonable to expect them to profit disproportionately from policies of preferential treatment applied merely according to membership in the minority group. It is also only reasonable to expect them to be differentially represented among the most qualified minority students. And if colleges and universities conceive of preferential treatment in terms of race or ethnic background only, rather than in terms of disadvantages actually suffered by the preferred individuals, then a fair application of meritocratic criteria to the pool of minority applicants can be expected to result in these same disproportions.

Richard Posner argues from census data that, since "most poor people are white," and since "most members of generally disadvantaged minorities are not poor," we can expect preferential admission by race to produce a common pattern of advantages for relatively affluent minority students over poor whites who are actually more disadvantaged. This is particularly so because we can "expect the nonpoor members of the minority groups to be over-represented, relative to the poor of their groups, among law school and other university applicants."[81]

81. Richard A. Posner, "The DeFunis Case and the Constitutionality of Preferential Treatment of Racial Minorities," in Philip B. Kurland, ed., *The Supreme Court Review 1974* (Chicago: University of Chicago Press, 1975), p. 15, n. 31.

Of course, once women are added to the pool of "minorities" (blacks, Indians, Orientals, and Hispanics) given group preference per se, the sheer number of relatively advantaged persons eligible for preferential treatment is expanded enormously. Thomas Sowell has calculated that:

> With the addition of women to the groups entitled to preferential (or "remedial") treatment, all the persons so entitled constitute about two-thirds of the total population of the United States.[82]

Even if minority group membership may serve usefully as an empirical proxy for actually suffered disadvantages in some empirical contexts, it would be difficult to defend the use of mere membership in minority groups when the groups are, together, so numerous as to cover two-thirds of the population.

The essential point is that practices of reverse discrimination applied merely according to native characteristics may benefit the relatively advantaged members of the designated group without substantially helping those who are truly deprived. Without administrative practices designed explicitly to guarantee their application to the disadvantaged, they stand open to the charge that they sacrifice merit without ensuring any significant gain in equality of life chances.

Of course, such practices do serve some worthy purposes. They may provide role models for other minority students, they may provide a critical mass of minority students in a given institution (raising the likelihood of survival in professional school for members of the minority group in general), and they may affect the development of aspirations on the part of other minority group members.[83] Yet these positive secondary efforts have to be balanced against negative ones; they may

82. Thomas Sowell, *Knowledge and Decisions* (New York: Basic Books, 1980), pp. 251–52.

83. See Greenawalt, "Judicial Scrutiny," in Gross, ed., *Reverse Discrimination,* pp. 228–32, and J. Harvey Wilkinson, *From Brown to Bakke: The Supreme Court and School Integration 1954–1978* (New York: Oxford University Press, 1979), pp. 274–89.

also have a major effect on the self-esteem of those admitted and a stigmatizing effect on all minority students, even those who would have been admitted without any preferential program.[84]

It is also worth noting that these programs may provide minority group members who are more likely to serve particular communities in their professional life. If the latter purpose were truly central though, it is arguable that special programs open to all races, for students willing to bind themselves to practice in particular areas or for particular groups, would serve the goal more effectively and in a nondiscriminatory way.[85] There is no doubt that nonminority group members can provide effective professional service to minority groups. In the United States, the history of civil rights cases and, indeed, the record of the Legal Services Corporation demonstrates this for the legal profession. The effective provision of professional services is, I believe, a less telling argument than the one based on role models and aspirations.

However these various secondary effects are evaluated, it is doubtful that they can be formulated strongly enough to justify a sacrifice in merit when that sacrifice is not accompanied by a gain in one of the other principles, such as equality of life chances. For unless preferential admissions were directed at those who had, themselves, suffered significant socioeconomic disadvantages, the preferential practices would be open to the charge that they render the competition unfair by making it turn on morally irrelevant native characteristics. Furthermore, while some of the secondary effects noted above may be significant—through providing role models for other students

84. See Thomas Sowell, *Black Education: Myths and Tragedies* (New York: McKay, 1972), p. 292, and Midge Decter, "On Affirmative Action and Lost Self-Respect," *The New York Times,* 6 July 1980.

85. Note that the University of California at Davis Medical School actually had a program of preference (only occasionally operational) for students who were prepared to practice in areas of northern California that were short of physicians. See Bakke v. Regents of University of California, 553 P.2d 1152, at 1157–58 (1976).

or potential professionals, or through raising the level of aspiration among minority group members—there is no reason to believe that these secondary effects will reach, much less, significantly affect, the disadvantaged so as to bear on equality of life chances. In the United States, where the disparity between the black middle class and the ghetto underclass has been growing disturbingly, visible benefits to the former may have little effect upon the latter.[86]

Some proponents of affirmative action would defend preferential treatment, even when those benefited were not disadvantaged or had not been subjected to previous discrimination. The Department of Justice, for example, in its amicus curiae brief in the *Bakke* case argued that "the consequences of discrimination are too complex to dissect on a case-by-case basis." Schools and employers "ought not to be confined to the choice of either ignoring the problem or attempting the Sisyphean task of discerning its importance on an individual basis." The separation of applicants on racial grounds alone, into separate admissions processes, was therefore held to be defensible because "when individual measurement would be impractical, a state may properly use categorical means."[87] A general category, race, provides a practical approximation to the results of a case-by-case assessment.

If this kind of approximation is the central justification, I have already noted reasons for questioning its applicability to practices of preferential treatment based merely on race. At least in highly competitive meritocratic processes (such as admission to professional schools), class, income, and other advantages will clearly affect the development of the relevant qualifications. Members of the designated racial or ethnic category who achieve the highest scores and other qualifica-

86. For a distressing account of the contrast between the ghetto underclass and the black middle class see the cover story, "The American Underclass: Destitute and Desperate in the Land of Plenty," in *Time* 110 (August 29, 1977): 14–27.

87. Brief of The United States of America as amicus curiae, *Bakke*, p. 56.

tions are likely to be disproportionately those who have not, themselves, come from relatively disadvantaged backgrounds. Hence the irony of the *DeFunis* case. Even a perfunctory investigation of income and family background would prevent preferential treatment from being awarded to relatively advantaged members of minority groups, instead of to the truly disadvantaged whose qualifications may appear less impressive. As I will show later, a further irony was that the program the court struck down in the *Bakke* case did include an effort to target preferential treatment toward relatively poor applicants. From our standpoint, the court's insensitivity to this factor was regrettable.

It is important to distinguish the issue of *compensation* for past discrimination from the issue of ameliorating developmental disadvantages in the present that may result from many other causes distinguishable from past discrimination. Low income, class background, inadequate housing, a broken home, or cultural or linguistic differences may be only tangentially related, if they are related at all, to previous acts of discrimination. Yet children growing up in homes affected by these disadvantages may be denied an equal life chance because their environments effectively inhibit the development of their talents and aspirations.

Efforts to correct these developmental disadvantages— through economic redistribution, intervention in the home environment, or provision of special compensatory schooling—do not require any references to past discrimination as the basis for their justification. A similar point can be made about efforts to equalize life chances despite the persistence of these developmental disadvantages, when the equalization would result from programs of preferential treatment for those who have actually suffered the disadvantages. In either case, such efforts could be justified by an aspiration to realize equality of life chances in order to bring about a fair system of individualistic competition. The equality of life chances principle would not distinguish cases where developmental disadvantages result from identifiable acts of discrimination from cases where the disadvantages result merely from socioeconomic inequality.

Yet perhaps compensation for past discrimination or other past injustice may be interpreted to require the kind of program I have been criticizing—preferential treatment for groups classified merely by race or other arbitrary native characteristics. However, it is the relatively poor and disadvantaged members of a given minority group—precisely those least likely to be benefited by preferential treatment applied merely by race in competitive contexts—who are likely to have a strong compensatory claim. Consider the compensatory argument that a person X is worse-off than he would otherwise have been because his parents were discriminated against, or because his distant forebears were enslaved. One approach would be the systematic investigation of historical and genealogical claims based on the background of each applicant, in order to arrive at some reasonable probabilistic construction of the required counterfactual; in other words, how well-off X might otherwise have likely been. Here the objection quoted above from the Justice Department brief in the *Bakke* case has considerable force. To investigate historical claims of compensation on behalf of each applicant surely would amount to an impractical burden in most of the social contexts where this issue has been raised.

On the other hand, race alone surely offers an inadequate proxy for identifying those subject to compensation since it is far from clear that the more advantaged members of a racial minority generally are worse-off than they would otherwise have been, were it not for discrimination practiced against their forebears in previous generations. A much more compelling probabilistic claim could be made on behalf of the ghetto underclass. Actual income and class background of one's parents, when combined with race or ethnic background, might provide a better, if still distant, approximation. It would more clearly identify victims of historical injustice than would race alone; it would identify present-day victims about whom it could be said that they would, in some sense, have been better off if their forebears had not suffered from discrimination or other injustice.

If this compensatory argument were pursued seriously, it would face two challenges. First, the list of groups previously subjected to discrimination is far broader than the groups now demanding compensatory benefits. Given the sad history of professional schools with respect to Jews, DeFunis himself might have had as valid a *historical* argument as did those admitted ahead of him. Consistent pursuit of the argument would produce a host of other historical ethnic claims—Irish, Polish and Italian, Catholic as well as Jewish, in addition to Hispanics, native Americans, and Orientals, to cite only the most obvious examples.

This Pandora's box is not fanciful. There has been public agitation for affirmative action to be extended to many other white ethnic groups presently underrepresented in American higher education, for example, Italians, Greeks, Slavs, and Poles.[88] Even narrow constructions of the compensatory argument have led to a proliferation of ethnic classifications. In its survey of post-Bakke professional school admissions, the Anti-Defamation League discovered one American law school that classified its applicants into the following ethnic and racial classifications:

(1) American Indian or Alaskan Native, (2) Chinese, (3) Filipino, (4) Hawaiian, (5) Korean, (6) Japanese, (7) Pacific Islander, "including Fijian, Micronesian, Samoan, Tahitian, Tongan, etc." (8) Other Asian, "including Cambodian, Sri Lankan, Laotian, Thai, Vietnamese, etc." (9) Mixed Asian and/or Pacific Islander, (10) Black, not of Hispanic origin, (11) Portuguese, (12) Puerto Rican, (13) Spanish, (14) Mixed Hispanic, (15) White, "including any persons hav-

88. Sindler, *Bakke, DeFunis, and Minority Admissions*, p. 266, and Wilkinson, *From Brown to Bakke*, pp. 268–69.

ing origin in any of the original peoples of North Africa, the Middle East, Indian Subcontinent or Europe (excluding Spain and Portugal)" and (16) Mixed Ethnic Background— "a combination of ethnic backgrounds which includes two or more of the five major categories—American Indian or Native Alaskan, Asian or Pacific Islander, Black, Hispanic and White."[89]

Furthermore, if historical claims about discrimination in this country provide the basis for compensatory programs, why should recently immigrated Hispanics benefit from preferential treatment? They can make no such historical claims unless the locus of responsibility is widened far beyond American domestic institutions.[90] While they may have a strong case on the basis of actually suffered developmental disadvantages, these recent immigrants do not have a similar claim based on compensation for historical injustice.

An additional complication arises for those subjected historically to discrimination whose descendants fail to share the characteristics that singled out members of an earlier generation for discrimination. Perhaps I am far worse-off now than I would otherwise have been, because my grandmother was discriminated against because she was a woman. It is clearly possible for the counterfactual standard to apply, namely, I would be better-off if she had not been discriminated against, even though I do not share the characteristic that singled her out for discrimination, namely, her sex.

There are equally perplexing issues about the locus of responsibility for paying the compensation. Some corporations and institutions guilty of past discrimination still exist. Others do not. However, many persons are now better-off than they would otherwise have been, just as others are now worse-off.

89. See Anti-Defamation League of B'nai B'rith, "A Study of post-Bakke Admissions Policies in Medical, Dental and Law Schools," *Rights* 10, no. 1 (Summer 1979): 11–12.

90. Wilkinson, *From Brown to Bakke*, p. 278.

Some present-day advantaged persons are now better-off because their parents, grandparents, or great-grandparents did not have to compete with groups discriminated against in previous generations. Others made fortunes out of slavery or other exploitative practices, fortunes that, in some cases, survive intact to the present day. If the compensatory arguments were to be taken seriously, some special responsibility for the payment of compensation might be placed on these persons, were it possible to identify them nonarbitrarily.

In addition to the proliferation of claims, there is a challenge of a different sort also facing the compensatory argument. An individual, X, is supposed to be compensated by returning him to the level of well-being he would have reached, were it not for some identifiable injustice in the past committed against his forebears. In tracing back through the generations, however, it soon becomes clear that for many of the cases for which we might think compensation was owed, X would not have existed, were it not for the injustice in question. In our construction of the counterfactual, the historical chain of events following from the hypothetical nonoccurrence of the stated injustice, it is quite reasonable to suppose that we would find no individual, X, existing in the alternative world thus envisaged.[91]

If Kunta Kinte, Alex Haley's ancestor portrayed in *Roots*, had not been brutally kidnapped and sold as a slave, there is virtually no likelihood that the author of *Roots* would have come to exist in the twentieth century. The mating and reproduction of each generation, in turn, would have depended on a host of contingent circumstances. A different genealogical line would have been created were the chain to have been broken at any point, for instance, if a parent, grandparent, or great-

91. I have been influenced in this argument by Derek Parfit's work on identity and the moral claims of possible persons. See the literature cited in nn. 40 and 41, chapter 2. I have also benefited from George Sher's "Ancient Wrongs and Modern Rights," *Philosophy and Public Affairs* 10 no. 1 (Winter 1981): 3–17.

grandparent were to have mated with someone else. Kunta Kinte's descendants would have been native Africans, perhaps residents of Juffure (Kunta Kinte's village in West Africa), had the initial injustice not occurred.

The particular circumstances of slavery in one generation, freedom in another, determined a host of contingencies affecting the choice of mates and the identities of each generation in turn. Any realistic construction of an alternative world in which the enslavement of a given person X's ancestors had not occurred would not be likely to include X, on whose behalf present compensation is being demanded. How then, could compensation for injustices to previous generations satisfy the strict notion of compensation and, thereby, return X to the level of well-being X would have enjoyed, had the injustice in the past not occurred?

Or, to take a simpler case, while my grandmother may have suffered from sex discrimination and while certain disadvantages to her descendants may have causally followed, she would clearly have had different descendants had it not been for the sex discrimination. If we imagine her pursuing a professional career rather than that of a full-time housewife, she would surely have had fewer than the five children she did have; she might not have had any at all and the timing of her children would surely have been different. If I attempt to envision the alternative world that would have resulted, had discrimination not occurred, I cannot plausibly locate myself in it.

Perhaps this strict criterion of compensation should be loosened. Perhaps X should be compensated to the level of well-being that some closely related, identifiable person X' would have reached, had the injustice not occurred. A viable theory of individualistic compensation would require well-developed criteria for identifying X' in the counterfactual world—for identifying, for example, a descendant of Kunta Kinte who would have come to exist had the injustice not occurred and for comparing the level of well-being achieved by Alex Haley (before the writing of *Roots*) with that of the alternative hypothetical descendant of his ancestors.

There are enormous challenges, both theoretical and empirical, facing the development and application of such a theory of compensation for intergenerational injustice. Perhaps an adequate version of this kind of theory might be developed, although my argument here will not depend on it. I need only note that were such a theory to be developed, it would have implications that parallel, in essential respects, the conclusion reached above. Plausible constructions of the required counterfactuals would lead to the same objection presented earlier to preferential treatment applied merely to racial or ethnic categories. Since there are clear pressures, in competitive contexts, to admit the most qualified members of the specified racial or ethnic groups, the most qualified members are likely to come from relatively more advantaged rather than less advantaged backgrounds. Yet it is precisely the relatively more advantaged about whom it can least plausibly be said that they are worse-off than they would have been (or than identifiable relatives would have been) had not injustices occurred to previous generations. Similarly, it is the less advantaged for whom the counterfactual claim is most plausible and for whom the harm (the gap between their present position and the counterfactual supposition) is likely to be greatest (or at least far greater than any claim that might be lodged on behalf of the more advantaged).

Hence, the compensatory argument, like the argument from developmental disadvantages, leads us to reject preferential treatment merely applied to racial or ethnic categories and instead leads to requirements that preferential treatment, if it is to be adopted at all, should be directed only toward the disadvantaged. Income, class background, and whatever other information could be handled administratively in a reasonable manner would have to be taken into account. In addition, if it were possible to identify more precise compensatory claims for each individual such efforts would clearly be supported by this kind of argument.

One central difference between the compensatory argument for past discrimination and the argument from developmental disadvantages in the present is that the latter would clearly require special efforts for all persons now suffering from specifiable and extreme disadvantages, regardless of their racial or ethnic background. For example, preferential treatment for poor whites would be required if the principal effort were to overcome developmental disadvantages in the present in order to equalize life chances. By contrast, the compensatory argument for past discrimination would not, presumably, include poor whites. It would, by contrast, include consideration of racial and ethnic classifications for all groups subjected to past discrimination; these classifications would provide part of the basis for identifying those now eligible for compensation according to some counterfactual consideration of how well-off they would have been (or how well-off appropriately related persons would have been) had the discrimination not occurred.

It is worth noting that both of these versions of preferential treatment targeted toward the disadvantaged—the version aimed at compensation for past injustice and the version aimed at ameliorating present developmental disadvantages—should satisfy our proposed minimum condition. In either case, the sacrifice in merit would clearly be accompanied by a gain in one of our other principles, in this case, equality of life chances. Such policies would benefit persons from disadvantaged backgrounds who could not otherwise realistically aspire to the higher positions. Of course, satisfaction of our minimum condition, no sacrifice in one of our principles without an improvement in one or more of the others,[92] does not settle the question of how these conflicting claims are to be weighed or balanced one against the other. It does, however, remove the easy objection to the mistargeting of benefits (to the nondisadvantaged) from preferential treatment merely applied to racial

92. An improvement in one or more of the other principles, or an improvement in some other morally relevant factor that would then have to be argued for. See the earlier discussion of the minimum condition at the beginning of this section.

or ethnic categories, in competitive meritocratic contexts. While our minimum condition does not resolve the general problem by any means, it is far from trivial in its implications for actual policy.

Let me return to my original thought experiment. The point of imagining attempts to realize all three principles under ideal conditions was to argue that simultaneous commitment to fulfilling all three amounted to an incoherent ideal under the best conditions that might realistically be assumed for a large industrial society, provided that background conditions of inequality were left in place.

Within the liberal framework of individualistic competition, the departure from ideal theory required to approach the actual American policy context raises the problem of what would be necessary, at any point in time, to implement "a fair competition among individuals for unequal positions" when the immediately relevant recent history has produced assignments of persons to positions that were unfair because they were based on discrimination.

The question is whether a person is worse-off than he ought to have been in the competition because one or more of the principles of fair competition being implemented (merit or equality of life chances) has been violated in the past. As we have seen, compensation for previous violations of merit, that is, discrimination, may require present violations of merit, that is, preferential treatment. Similarly, attempts to achieve equality of life chances (with the autonomy of the family in place) would require sacrifice of merit (whether under ideal or under less than ideal conditions). In either case, the benefits of defensible preferential treatment must be directed at those individuals who have suffered from past discrimination or from unequal developmental conditions. Preferential treatment when targeted carefully in that way would be compatible with the basic aim of implementing a fair competition among individuals for unequal positions. Either by compensating for previous violations of merit or by achieving greater equality of life chances (or both), such specially designed programs of preferential treatment would lead to an improved realization of one or more of the principles in this individualistic framework.

By contrast, it would not be an improvement in fair individualistic competition to sacrifice merit, through programs of preferential treatment based merely on race or ethnic background, without also accomplishing greater equality of life chances. In empirical contexts where they produce substantial mistargeting, such programs do not compensate individuals for past violations, nor do they contribute directly to realizing in the present either of the principles of fair competition (merit or equality of life chances).[93] Their secondary effects on the framework of individualistic competition—provision of role models, effects on aspirations—are not likely to substantially affect the life chances of the less advantaged. And they come at the cost of a severe sacrifice in merit. As we shall see in the next chapter, one would have to depart strikingly from our original liberal framework of individualistic competition in order to justify such programs.

93. Of course, in some empirical contexts preferential treatment by race may not turn out to produce substantial mistargeting because virtually all members of the group, even the most disadvantaged, have the requisite skills. That is why the objection developed here was restricted to highly competitive meritocratic contexts. My objection is to the mistargeting phenomenon and not to the use of preferential treatment per se.

4. FAIRNESS, GROUP COMPENSATION, AND EQUALITY: RESPONSES TO THE TRILEMMA

In the last chapter, my central claim was that given background conditions of inequality, commitment to both principles of equal opportunity produces an incoherent ideal when it is combined with our customary commitment of the autonomy of the family. The principles of merit, equal life chances, and family autonomy conflict according to a systematic pattern. Like a three-cornered stool with only two legs available to prop it up, this combination of commitments is unsupportable, even as an ideal for guiding public policy under the best conditions that might realistically be imagined for a modern industrial society. One strategy would be to accept one of the three unpleasant options in the trilemma—accepting the required sacrifice in merit, equal life chances, or the autonomy of the family. Another strategy would be to reformulate either our basic commitment to these notions of equal opportunity or our basic commitment to the autonomy of the family. The only remaining alternative compatible with these commitments would be to relax the assumption of background conditions of inequality and, hence, to prescribe equality of outcomes rather than merely equality of opportunities.

This last alternative confirms our earlier conclusion with respect to the family. Equal opportunity, far from being the weakly reformist notion sometimes alleged,[1] is a startlingly

1. See Schaar, "Equality of Opportunity and Beyond," in Pennock and Chapman, eds., *Nomos IX Equality*. See also Bowles and Gintis, *Schooling in Capitalist America*, for a critique of the legitimating function performed by those versions of "equal opportunity" compatible with a capitalist economy.

radical idea. Either it would require systematic intrusions into the family and a vast revision in the way of life we commonly take for granted, or it would require the even more radical reforms required for the systematic elimination of both social and economic background inequalities. In either case, equal opportunity could be fully implemented only at a considerable cost in liberty—either in the private sphere of liberty at issue in the family, or in the liberties of property, contract, and employment that would have to be infringed in order to maintain equality of outcomes.

I interpreted the principles of merit and equal life chances as essential components of the basic competitive assumption— that there should be *a fair competition among individuals for unequal positions in society.* Let us consider possible revisions in the crucial components of this definition. These may be identified as: "fairness," "competition," "individuals," and "unequal positions." I will consider these in the sections below.

4.1 Fairness and Merit   Notions of fairness were involved explicitly in the arguments for merit and equal life chances. The principle of merit is, itself, the expression of a kind of procedural fairness. More demanding notions of "background fairness" can be employed to support equal life chances. Various modifications of these notions of fairness might be introduced in order to avoid any initial commitment to the principles yielding our trilemma.

Recall the earlier definition:

THE PRINCIPLE OF MERIT: *There should be widespread procedural fairness in the evaluation of qualifications for positions.*

The limited implications of equal opportunity with respect to race are probed in Edwin Dorn's *Rules and Racial Equality* (New Haven: Yale University Press, 1979). See my discussion of some of those contentions below.

And by qualifications I meant: criteria that are job-related in that they fairly can be interpreted as indicators of competence or motivation for an individual's performance in a given position.

If this definition of qualifications were to be revised so that membership in a given race, family, class, or ethnic group could, in itself, count as a qualification to be considered impartially in the process of meritocratic competition, then our trilemma of equal opportunity could be avoided. For then both equal life chances and merit, in the revised sense determined by such a new definition of qualifications, could be fully instituted without the autonomy of the family being affected. Despite the unequal development of talents and other qualifications protected by family autonomy, qualifications could be defined in such a way that persons could be routed into the higher positions in the precise proportions required by equality of life chances. By redefining qualifications, the resulting principle of merit could be formulated to mirror the precise effects of the kind of preferential treatment considered earlier. This new definition simply would make explicit the new terms of competition.

It would be difficult, however, to consider the new competition a fair one in the same sense. Family background, race, or sex do not support the same justificatory burdens of job relevance as do competence and motivation. Furthermore, they are not earned; they are not subject to the same process of competitive acquisition. And if technological innovations permitted them to be acquired—permitting one to change races, for example, as sexes are now sometimes changed, that would not increase equality of life chances for native members of such groups for it might only permit newly altered proxies to take advantaged places instead.

The notion of merit, as originally defined, captured a claim to procedural fairness that carefully insulated the assignment process from factors that were irrelevant to performance in the positions to be filled. One could view the results of meritocratic competition as merited or entitled by competitive efforts at acquisition and then by fair evaluation of the results. Redefining merit so as to explicitly include race or family background would constitute a disturbing departure from this position for most liberals. One cannot earn one's race or family background in the same way that one is supposed to earn the qualifications evaluated by merit.

Perhaps the principle of merit needs to be sacrificed in order to fulfill other important goals such as equal life chances or compensatory claims for past injustice. But the cost of sacrificing the principle only would be obscured were qualifications to be redefined so that merit could include membership in a given race, class, or ethnic group.[2]

This redefinition of merit sacrifices the claim to procedural fairness bult into the original principle, but might be held to serve background fairness.[3] Let us now turn to the alternative strategy of sacrificing background fairness but maintaining the commitment to procedural fairness. Suppose I interpreted "a fair competition for unequal positions" (our initial "fair competition" assumption) to require only adherence to merit in our original sense?

To reduce equal opportunity to the limited procedural requirements defined by merit would constitute, I believe, a drastic and disturbing truncation of an otherwise inspiring ideal. Such a limited conception is open to the obvious objection that is would be satisfied even by the limited reforms

2. Justice Powell's opinion in *Bakke* is a step in this direction; race may be considered explicitly as "one element to be weighed fairly against other elements in the selection process." See Alfred A. Slocum, ed., *Allan Bakke versus Regents of the University of California* 6 vols. (Dobbs Ferry: Oceana, 1978), "Opinion, Majority by Mr. Justice Powell," 6:355. See Anti-Defamation League, "A Study of post-Bakke Admissions Policies," for evidence that race has been commonly treated since as a major qualification in its own right.

3. Depending on how much weight mere membership in a given race or class were accorded in such a new definition of merit, this strategy might increase equality of life chances. But it would do so in the same way that the second option in our trilemma did so, by sacrificing the claim to procedural fairness offered by merit in our original sense.

exemplified in our imaginary warrior society. Recall that in the warrior society a competition was instituted to determine the best warriors in order to regulate admission to the upper strata. Children of the present warriors continued to dominate the competition because they were well-nourished, while children from other strata verged on starvation. There is no doubt, however, that the competition did, indeed, select the best warriors. Yet the specter, let us imagine, of 300 pound Sumo wrestlers vanquishing 90 pound weaklings offers a disturbing ideal of equal opportunity. The reason, of course, is that grossly unequal developmental conditions in this simplified case (differential nourishment) yield similarly unequal life chances. The conditions underlying a competition can be judged unfair if we can predict how people will do in it merely from knowledge of the strata into which they were born. Hence, the notion of background fairness that yields equal life chances seems just as essential as did the notion of procedural fairness that yielded merit. Sacrificing either principle would produce a truncated and inadequate ideal of equal opportunity. Both types of fairness, as I have interpreted them, seem to provide essential components of the liberal doctrine of equal opportunity.

4.2 Competition and Lotteries   Each of these departures from our earlier analysis of a fair competition would require a disturbing revision of liberal assumptions. Perhaps, instead of modifying notions of fairness, we might modify notions of competition. A lottery system might be formulated to preserve procedural fairness. Unbiased by morally irrelevant factors such as race, sex, class, or family background, it could be instituted to achieve equal life chances. In that way, it would offer a strategy for realizing both procedural and background fairness without requiring the sacrifice in liberty identified by the autonomy of the family. This strategy is an example of the kind of revision of fundamental assumptions that would evade our trilemma by abandoning one of the central principles, merit, and replacing it with an alternative claim to procedural fairness.

In this kind of lottery system, persons would be regarded as passive recipients of statistically equal chances rather than as active participants in a competition. No person's actual behavior would affect where he or she would end up. The result would represent a severe challenge to liberty in employment although it would not affect the private sphere of liberty involved in the family. If I wanted to be a doctor but the lottery required that I be an auto mechanic, or if I wanted to be a lawyer but the lottery required that I be an orchestra conductor, my liberty to seek and compete for employment would be forfeited by the lottery system. Concurrently, there would also be a severe cost in efficiency. If people were assigned regardless of aptitude and developed competence, some gross mismatchings could be presumed to result. My assignment to be an orchestra conductor would surely constitute a somewhat fanciful example of this kind of mismatching. I speculate that no amount of on-the-job training could ever be expected to lead to my performing that function competently. Meanwhile, many a nascent conductor might be assigned to positions where I would blossom.

Of course, we might also imagine a pure lottery system combined with provisions for trades or even a market. The sacrifice in competence and efficiency again would be severe. Imagine X, who has always wanted to be a conductor but who has no talent in the field whatsoever, trading his lottery entitlement for mine. He might be happier in the position than I would but no improvement in competence need result. And if a market so as to allow side payments were permitted (or if a black market in lottery tickets were not prevented), then background inequalities would enable those who were willing and able to spend more to compromise the principle of equal life chances. It would permit the rich, or their children, to buy up the most desirable lottery entitlements.

Any market in lottery entitlements, or any system permitting trades in positions, could be expected to undermine the equality of life chances produced by the lottery initially. Some people will be better traders or have better connections, and some entitlements will be far more tradeable (depending on the distribution of preferences and skills). Even if explicit side payments are ruled out, a host of arbitrary factors would permit some people to parlay their lottery entitlements into much better than equal life chances, if trades on markets were permitted.

On the other hand, when this lottery notion is interpreted strictly so as to realize equal life chances, it offers a stark contrast to the liberty of employment presumed by the principle of merit. Merit permits each of us to participate actively in the process of assignment. We are free to decide what we wish to compete for; we are free to attempt to acquire the appropriate qualifications (restricted only, I assume, by meritocratic competition for the opportunities to undergo the requisite training).

The lottery, by contrast, would substitute equal *chances* for equal *opportunities;* it would substitute equal chances, passively, to receive positions for equal opportunities, actively, to compete for those positions. The lottery would, admittedly, offer procedural fairness by ruling out discrimination or preferential treatment based on race, sex, class, or ethnic or family origin. Because it would also be insensitive to individual competence and preference, however, it would require sacrifices in both efficiency and liberty of employment—values that are both promoted by the principle of merit.

Thus the lottery might achieve equal chances in a procedurally fair way, but at a severe cost in individual initiative and liberty. People would become passive recipients of equal chances rather than active seekers of equal opportunities. If taken seriously, the lottery notion would require a drastic departure from our basic competitive assumption. Although it offers a strategy for evading the trilemma, it does so, I believe, at a cost that most liberals would find deeply disturbing. While it must be counted among the theoretically possible solutions, the costs in both efficiency and liberty render it a less-than-inspiring ideal for liberal theory.

4.3 Group Competition and Compensation   Another strategy for avoiding the trilemma would be to relax the assumption that the fair competition must take place among individuals. If it were conceptualized as a group competition, then there would be a defense for precisely those policies of preferential treatment we objected to earlier.

The notion of a fair competition among groups leads naturally to claims that members of the group should get a representative, or even proportional, share of the desirable social positions. If blacks, Hispanics, or American Indians represent, respectively, X_1, X_2, and X_3 percent of the total population, it is natural to question why they do not also constitute the same percentages in any given desirable profession, class, or ranked social position. And if the reply is based on reference to their percentages in the relevant qualified pools of applicants, then the same question can be raised about group percentages in each of the preceding steps in the sorting process. The focus changes to the percentages of high school and college graduates, or applicants to professional schools, who turn out to be black, Hispanic, or American Indian.[4]

Receiving less than their proportionate share in any of these cases provides groups with a basis for claims that the terms of competition among groups must, in some way, be unfair. Perhaps there is discrimination or some systematic inequality

4. See Dorn, *Rules and Racial Equality*, chapter 4, where this group percentage notion is offered as an ideal for racial and ethnic equality. He does not, however, mean it to be applied too rigidly to each particular occupation. If blacks do not comprise "exactly 11 percent avocado farmers or psychiatrists," he would not have cause for complaint (p. 126). Rather, the focus should be on substantial departures from proportionate representation. See also, for example, Sindler, *Bakke, DeFunis, and Minority Admissions.* pp. 35, 55–57, and 266–67 for some other examples of group proportion calculations.

in causal conditions. Or perhaps cultural differences have an effect on the development of aspirations. Whatever the root cause of disproportionate shares, the notion of a fair competition among groups, rather than among individuals, would lead naturally to some redress via a closer allotment of proportional shares. Hence, an argument would follow for a strong version of preferential treatment for members of the group.

As long as fairness claims are conceptualized among groups, rather than among individuals, there would be no compelling claim for any commitment to the principle of assignment by merit. The latter notion was defined, of course, in terms of individual qualifications. Assignment by group membership might seem unfair to individuals but it could be managed so as to achieve a recognizable notion of fairness among groups, namely, each group receiving what is, in some sense, held to be its "representative" or "fair" share of the desirable social positions.

Such a departure from our basic assumption about competition among individuals would avoid the trilemma by avoiding the commitment, in the first place, to the principle of merit that is sacrificed by preferential treatment. Owen Fiss offers a particularly well-developed and influential example of arguments for the explicit consideration of groups. He reasons that:

> There are natural classes or social groups in American society and blacks are such a group. Blacks are viewed as a group; they view themselves as a group; their identity is in large part determined by membership in the group; their social status is linked to the status of the group; and much of our action, institutional and personal, is based on these perspectives.[5]

5. Owen M. Fiss, "Groups and the Equal Protection Clause," in Cohen, Nagel, and Scanlon, eds., *Equality and Preferential Treatment*, p. 125. Fiss also includes two conditions that must be satisfied by such a social group: "(1) It is an *entity*, . . . you can talk about the group without reference to the particular individuals who happen to be its members at any one moment. (2) There is also a condition of *interdependence*. The identity and well-being of the members of the group and the identity and well-being of the group are linked." (p. 125).

Fiss argues that when this conception of blacks as a "social group" is combined with a realization of their long-term status as an "underclass," the basis is laid for preferential treatment according to group characteristics. He mentions two crucial factors:

> One is that blacks are very badly off, probably our worst-off class (in terms of material well-being second only to the American Indians), and in addition they have occupied the lowest rung for several centuries. In a sense, they are America's perpetual underclass. It is both of these characteristics—the relative position of the group and the duration of the position—that make efforts to improve the position of the group defensible.[6]

Fiss considers preferential treatment (or, more generally, "redistribution") as justified by two possible arguments. One is compensation, the other is the ethical objection to "castes." Consider the first:

> This redistribution may be rooted in a theory of compensation—blacks as a group were put in that position by others and the redistributive measures are owed to the group as a form of compensation.[7]

This notion of group compensation would face the difficulties we encountered earlier with individualistic compensation. It is worth noting, however, that the identity issue does not arise in precisely the same way. While it is arguable that a particular present-day black would not be here (or would not exist at all) were it not for injustices committed in the past, (hence, attempting to compensate him to the level he would have reached were it not for those injustices raises the identity problem, namely, that he would not otherwise have been) the same cannot be said for blacks as a group. The persons to whom the injustices were committed would, in general, have

6. Ibid., p. 127.
7. Ibid.

had other descendants and the well-being of that alternative group can be considered in the required counterfactual.

Of course, those descendants might not have been Americans had it not been for the initial act of enslavement and transportation to America. For these purposes, however, we can distinguish the initial injustice committed against blacks in bringing them to this country from all of the subsequent injustices committed against them, once here. It should be clear that the latter were so severe as to provide a basis for compensatory arguments, were such arguments to be admitted at all, without any necessity to take account of the former as well.

At first glance, then, group compensation appears to evade the identity problem because the same group (if not the same individuals) could be presumed to exist in the counterfactual world that would have arisen had the injustices for which compensation is being demanded not taken place. The problem of maintaining individual identity in the counterfactual world does not appear to apply to the group.

However, the problem still does arise but in a different way. While there would still be American blacks, it is arguable that had the injustices to their ancestors not occurred, American blacks would not constitute a social group in the same sense. Without a legacy of slavery, discrimination, and other injustices, blacks might not constitute a social group or "natural class" in Fiss's sense. In other words, were it not for these previous injustices, it is likely that their identity and status would not be linked, as they are now, to their group membership. It is likely that they would not satisfy one of the necessary conditions for being a social group, a condition Fiss calls "interdependence":

> Members of the group identify themselves—explain who they are—by reference to their membership in the group; and their well-being or status is in part determined by the well-being or status of the group.[8]

8. Ibid., p. 125.

Were it not for a history of injustice and discrimination rendering Americans color conscious, blacks might very well not constitute an "interdependent" group in this sense. Absent such a tragic history, the mere existence of physical differences surely would not be enough to fulfill this condition. Blue-eyed persons are physically distinguishable from the rest of the population, but they do not define their identities in terms of eye color. Neither do they view their well-being or status as determined, even in part, by the well-being or status of other blue-eyed persons. On the other hand, we might speculate that had there been a history of discrimination and injustice directed at blue-eyed persons, consciousness of eye color might have grown to the point that blue-eyed persons would have come to constitute a social group in Fiss's "interdependent" sense.

Similarly, if we were to embark upon the admittedly difficult task of imagining the alternative world (or worlds) that might have occurred had injustices to blacks not been committed, it is arguable that we might find a society in which race functioned somewhat the way eye color does now.[9] In a racially neutral society, blacks would not constitute a social group or natural class. Their status, identity, and welfare would not be tied to their group membership. Therefore, but for the injustices for which compensation is being advocated, the group to be compensated would not exist as a social group. And in this way, we see that a theory of intergenerational group compensation faces a version of the identity problem— the group cannot be returned to the level of well-being it would have enjoyed, had the injustices not occurred, because had the injustices not occurred, it would not have been a group, at least in the same strict sense.

One might contend that compensating the group, per se, in the alternative world is not as important as compensating the

9. I take the eye color analogy from Richard A. Wasserstrom, *Philosophy and Social Issues: Five Studies* (Notre Dame: University of Notre Dame, 1980), p. 15.

individuals who would have comprised the group. But this would return us to individualistic compensation, a principle for which identity issues arise even more dramatically. There is a clear basis for claiming that the particular individuals who comprise the group in the world actually resulting, in part, from previous injustices, would not exist in the alternative, hypothetical world that would have resulted had the injustices to past generations not occurred.[10] Similarly, the individuals we would find in an alternative world, that lacked our present social groups, would not be the same individuals as the members of the group for which compensation is now being advocated.

Because we find neither the same group nor the same individuals in the alternative world, identifying the level of well-being that would have resulted had the injustices not occurred becomes problematical. Group compensation arguments face the challenge of providing a theory of group identity for such counterfactuals. In what sense ought we to compensate groups for their loss of well-being, had injustices not occurred, when had it not been for the injustices, neither the group nor the particular individuals within it would likely exist today?

One kind of compensation argument that might be envisioned would avoid this identity problem in formulating the counterfactual. It is arguable that some forms of existence are so terrible that it would be better never to have existed at all rather than experience such misery. If an individual experiences so deprived an existence that we can plausibly say of him, "it would have been better, had he never been born," then his nonexistence provides a coherent construction of the counterfactual.[11]

10. For some interesting calculations showing how even small divergences in population in one generation will produce vast differences in the population membership of later generations, see Thomas Schwartz, "Obligations to Posterity," in Sikora and Barry, *Obligations to Future Generations*, pp. 3–13, especially pp. 5–6.

11. See chapter 3, n. 31.

Two points should be made about this variant of the compensation argument. First, although it avoids the identity argument, it does so in a manner that renders it similarly difficult to determine the appropriate benchmark for compensation. What is the level of actual well-being that corresponds to nonexistence? The persons in question are so miserable that bringing them into existence to live such a life was a form of harm—a harm they should be compensated for by returning them to a level of well-being that somehow corresponds to the one they would have experienced, if the harm had not occurred. But if the harm had not occurred, they would not have experienced anything at all, since they would not have existed. Death, the interruption of an existence already begun, should not be confused with the nonexistence of those who were never born (or conceived). It should be clear that intergenerational compensation arguments are as problematical in this construction as they are in the variants already considered.

A second point about this version of the compensation argument is that it only supports a compensatory claim on behalf of those who actually suffer such an extraordinarily miserable existence. Hence it would not support compensation for persons identified merely on the basis of group characteristics such as race or ethnic origin, unless empirical circumstances made it reasonable to suppose that virtually all members of the group actually suffered, themselves, an existence so miserable that the counterfactual claim applied to them—namely that it would have been better had they never been born.

Hence the strategy of tying compensation to hypothetical nonexistence is not only subject to some extraordinary difficulties, it also lends little support to group compensatory arguments in the present context. And as we have seen, any viable theory of group compensation would face the identity issue in the distinctive version that arises for groups. Let us suppose, however, that this difficulty is somehow overcome. Suppose that advocates of group compensation provide us with a theory of group identity for counterfactual worlds such that we can determine the hypothetical level of well-being that a group, or at least a collection of persons, would have reached, had it not been for the injustices committed to previous members of an identifiable group.

Were it available, such a theory would permit us to determine the amount of compensation owed, or at least, the level of well-being that we ought to attempt to bring to the group being compensated. However, such a theory would still require a justification for compensating all present members of the group (defined, for example, on racial or ethnic grounds) rather than merely particular persons who had, themselves, suffered some deprivation requiring compensation.

One rationale for such a policy of group compensation might be found in the interdependence condition proposed by Fiss as part of the definition of a social group or natural class. Remember this condition provides that the "well-being or status" of any member of the group is "in part determined by the well-being or status of the group." Depending on the extent of this interdependence, it might be argued that improvements in the well-being or status of the whole group might be interpreted as improvements to the individual members, since the individual status or well-being of each member is, by hypothesis, "in part determined by the well-being or status of the group." Of course, the issue turns on what is meant by "in part." A quite extraordinary degree of interdependence would be required were this condition to provide the rationale for group compensation.

Would any of us seriously maintain that members of the "perpetual underclass" (to use Fiss's term) are compensated for past injustice by policies of preferential treatment that do not affect their own life chances directly, but that affect, instead, the life chances of other persons who are members of the same group? The average or total level of well-being of a given racial or ethnic group could be improved by such policies of preferential treatment. However, if those policies are not directed so as to help precisely those persons for whom individualistic compensation might be demanded (those who have, themselves, actually suffered significant deprivations), then any claim that the persons left out are compensated through "interdependence" becomes implausible. Whatever satisfaction or pride unemployed ghetto blacks might take in the visible income and status of upper-middle class blacks, it must be quite paltry compared to what they would feel were they to reach the same positions themselves. It is unrealistic to expect the interdependent aspect of group welfare functions to make up for the fact that compensation policies based merely on group membership are not targeted so as to reach those who have, themselves, suffered greatly from the injustices for which compensation is being demanded.

Such a theory of group compensation, then, must depend on an assumption about the appropriateness of groups, rather than individuals, as the unit of analysis such that the group as a whole can be regarded as having been compensated for a past injustice even when many of the individuals actually receiving compensation never suffered from the injustice, and even when many of the individuals who have suffered from the injustice have not actually received compensation. According to such a theory, so long as the group as a whole is sufficiently better-off, mistargeting of the compensation to individuals would not undermine the claim that compensation for past injustices has been fulfilled.

Unlike individual compensation, group compensation theories would be vulnerable to a basic objection now commonly offered against utilitarianism—the objection that they fail to take account of the separateness of persons. Just as utilitarianism may tolerate extreme disadvantages to some persons provided that enough others are benefited, this form of group compensation would tolerate persistent injustices to some persons, provided that other persons (who have not themselves been victimized but who are members of the same group) receive sufficient benefits. Just as utilitarianism might even justify slavery under some possible conditions (provided that the rest of the society receives sufficient aggregate utility from the practice), the group compensation argument could lead us to tolerate the persisting effects of slavery and injustice imposed on some persons, on the condition that other members of the same group receive sufficient benefits.[12]

An aggregative principle, as noted in chapter two, must be indifferent between differing distributions of goods or welfare provided that the total (or with population held constant, the average) is the same under the differing distributions being considered. A policy of group compensation, merely concerned with total or average levels of welfare, income, or status—for example, for blacks or Hispanics as groups—would have this same aggregative feature.

As long as preferential policies raised the average or total level of the group, that would be justification enough according to this kind of principle. How the benefits of preferential treatment were distributed within the minority group being compensated would not affect the basic issue. This is an implication that Fiss accepts forthrightly. He considers the possibility that programs of preferential treatment might be administered so as to avoid favoring "rich blacks." Such an exclusion is not appropriate, we are told: "wholly apart from considerations of administrative convenience, the decision not to exclude the rich blacks (even once identified) can be justified."[13] He explains:

> The claim is that the preference of the rich blacks may be justified in terms of improving the position of the group. *Even if the blacks preferred happen to be rich, a benefit abounds to the group as a whole.* Members of that group have obtained these positions of power, prestige and influ-

12. For the wide influence of this "distinctively modern criticism of utilitarianism," see H. L. A. Hart's discussion of the separateness of persons argument in "Between Utility and Rights," in Alan Ryan, ed., *The Idea of Freedom: Essays in Honor of Isaiah Berlin* (Oxford: Oxford University Press, 1979) p. 78.
13. Fiss, "Groups and the Equal Protection Clause," p. 140.

ence that they otherwise might not have and to that extent the status of the group is improved.[14]

Preferring poor persons, Fiss adds, would not help "the poor conceived as a group—the preferred individual merely leaves the group," presumably, because he is no longer poor. Fiss's conclusion:

> Even if there were group benefits entailed in a preference for the poor, certainly legislators or administrators are entitled to rank the improvement of blacks as a group as a social goal of first importance, more important than elevating the poor conceived as a social group.[15]

A group preference principle, like the one advocated by Fiss, has the property that as long as the position of blacks, taken generally as a group, is improved, it does not matter whether the particular persons benefited are the already advantaged, the "rich blacks," or members of the ghetto underclass. This kind of group preference seems particularly open to objection when it is justified by a notion of compensation for past injustice. Consider, for example, the contrast between such a policy and German efforts after World War II to provide restitution to the victims of Nazi persecution. According to a 1949 West German law, these efforts,

> provided compensation for (a) loss of life, (b) damage to limb or health, (c) deprivation of liberty, (d) damage to property and possessions and (e) damage to economic advancement, to persons persecuted in Germany because of political conviction, or on racial, religious or ideological grounds.[16]

---

14. Ibid., emphasis has been added.
15. Ibid.
16. These provisions are quoted in Derek L. Phillips, *Equality, Justice and Rectification: An Exploration in Normative Sociology* (New York: Academic Press, 1979), p. 285.

Of course, Jewish survivors of the Holocaust were, over-whelmingly, the focus of this compensation program. Even the separate program of compensation paid to the state of Israel was justified in order "to assist in the integration of uprooted and destitute refugees from Germany and from lands formerly under German rule."[17]

It is important to note the careful routing of compensation to actual victims. Of course, this routing was not perfect. In 1956, for example, the criteria were loosened slightly to permit "probabilistic" causal connections between persecution and damage to health as a sufficient condition for compensation.[18] Likely victims were, in other words, given the benefit of the doubt.

The occasional mistargeting of benefits in individual cases that undoubtedly followed from the admission of probabilistic connections is, however, a minor matter compared to the massive mistargeting that could follow from any principle of group compensation, per se. Would any reasonable person have supported compensation to Jews, as such, regardless of their personal history of persecution? Would it not have been outra-geous if payments had been made, for example, to American Jews untouched by the Holocaust—in "compensation" for Nazi crimes—while many of the actual victims were uncom-pensated by the program?

Jews are, to a significant extent, an "interdependent" social group in Fiss's sense; yet the parallel principle of aggregative group compensation would have been an indefensible response to Nazi atrocities. Merely raising the average or total level of income or welfare, of Jews as a group, to the level they would have reached had it not been for the persecutions, would be an unacceptable substitute for compensating those individuals who had, themselves, suffered from Nazi atrocities. For one could raise the average or total level of the group without compensating any of the actual victims.

17. Ibid., p. 286.
18. Ibid., p. 285.

The same charge Rawls directs against utilitarianism can be directed against such an aggregative group principle: it "does not take seriously the distinction between persons."[19] It permits harm or deprivation to some persons to be tolerated for the sake of benefits to other persons, just as if there were one person or social entity that, somehow, experienced them all on behalf of the group. Nozick makes a similar argument against utilitarianism, an argument that we can apply, with equal appropriateness, to the group compensation principle:

> Individually, we each sometimes choose to undergo some pain or sacrifice for a greater benefit or to avoid a greater harm. . . . Why not, *similarly*, hold that some persons have to bear some costs that benefit other persons more, for the sake of the overall social good? But there is no *social entity* with a good that undergoes some sacrifice for its own good. There are only individual people, different individual people, with their own individual lives. Using one of these people for the benefit of others, uses him and benefits the others. Nothing more.[20]

As Nozick concludes about the person whose misery is tolerated for the sake of benefits to others: "that is the only life he has. He does not get some overbalancing good from his sacrifice, and no one is entitled to force this upon him."[21]

Group compensation, as contrasted to individual compensation, would permit benefits to some persons to count as compensation to other persons. Any theory that takes seriously the separateness of persons will be driven away from such a principle. It is individuals who experience these benefits and harms. The average or total levels prescribed by the group principle are statistical artifacts. One must look behind them to see whether those individuals who now benefit are the same

19. Rawls, *Theory of Justice,* p. 27.
20. Nozick, *Anarchy, State, and Utopia,* pp. 32–33.
21. Ibid., p. 33.

as those individuals who were previously harmed, if one wants to compensate for past injustice.

The notion of compensation to the victims of injustice, like the notion of punishment of the perpetrators of injustice, is most defensible when it meets an agent-specific requirement: claims that a given person should be either compensated or punished for a given injustice require reference to that particular agent's life history to establish that he—rather than merely someone similar to him in certain respects—had the alleged role in the injustice, as either victim or perpetrator. Principles of compensation, like principles of punishment, become extremely difficult to defend when they relax this agent-specific requirement and permit substitution of other members of a group for persons who played the actual role in the alleged injustice (whether that role be victim or perpetrator).

How would we react to the group principle if it were employed for punishment as well as for compensation? Would it not be extraordinarily objectionable if a criminal justice system were to view blacks, for example, as *interchangeable* for purposes of punishment—substituting any black for any other in the punishment of crimes committed by blacks? The blithe substitution of one person for another in the "justice" system that sent many Russians to the Gulag constitutes one of the most disturbing aspects of Solzhenitsyn's account of the Soviet prison camp system.[22] Persons are simply not substitutable for purposes of punishment, even when members of a group are

22. Aleksandr I. Solzhenitsyn, *The Gulag Archipelago: 1918–1956*, (New York: Harper and Row, 1973), chapters 1 and 3. For example: "By and large, the *Organs* had no profound reasons for their choice of whom to arrest and whom not to arrest. They merely had over-all assignments, quotas for a specific number of arrests. These quotas might be filled on an orderly basis or wholly arbitrarily. In 1937 a woman came to the reception room of the Novocherkassk NKVD to ask what she should do about the unfed unweaned infant of a neighbor who had been arrested. They said "Sit down, we'll find out." She sat there for two hours—whereupon they took her and tossed her into a cell. They had a total plan which had to be fulfilled in a hurry, and there was no one available to send out into the city—and here was this woman already in their hands!" (p. 11).

interdependent. It is, therefore, difficult to see why they should be interchangeable for purposes of compensation.

It is possible however, to argue for programs of preferential treatment for groups, as such, without basing those programs on a claim of compensation for past injustice. For example, Fiss offers a second, independent argument based on an ethical objection against "castes." We are told that "a redistributive strategy need not rest on this idea of compensation, it need not be backward looking." The alternative argument runs as follows:

> The redistributive strategy could give expression to an ethical view against caste, one that would make it undesirable for any social group to occupy a position of subordination for any extended period of time ... a variety of justifications can be offered and they need not incorporate the notion of compensation. Changes in the hierarchical structure of society—the elimination of caste—might be justified as a means of (a) preserving social peace; (b) maintaining the community as a community, that is, as one cohesive whole; or (c) permitting the fullest development of the individual members of the subordinated group who otherwise might look upon the low status of the group as placing a ceiling on their aspirations and achievements.[23]

I will not quarrel with Fiss's reasons for objecting to "castes." The instrumental goals just cited are worthy ones, although their precise connection to the persistence of castes would be open to debate. Nevertheless, the persistence of anything resembling a caste system seems unjust, in itself, regardless of how it relates to these other goals. Here, the interesting issue for our purposes is whether preferential treatment for social

23. Fiss "Groups and the Equal Protection Clause," p. 128. Fiss also makes an instrumental argument in terms of the distribution of political power (see pp. 128–29).

groups, in Fiss's sense, would constitute a remedy for the persistence of "castes" (at least to the degree this notion might apply to the United States) that is either necessary or effective.

Consider, for example, the result of implementing equal life chances, without any introduction of a preference for groups, as such. If equal life chances were realized, either through an equalization of developmental conditions, or through preferential policies targeted explicitly toward the disadvantaged, then a persisting racial underclass would be impossible. Over time, equal life chances would serve to randomly scatter any particular social group into positions throughout the society. Equal life chances between individuals would be an extraordinarily effective remedy for any persisting caste system. The lingering effects of a caste system could, in other words, be eliminated without any need to introduce a preference for groups.

Edwin Dorn, in his provocative recent book, *Rules and Racial Equality*, offers an apparent counterargument to this latter claim. He defines "equal opportunity" in a sense very close to the notion of equal life chances emphasized here:

> What equal opportunity means is that both A and B have the same a priori probability of receiving the good [whose distribution is in question]. Put differently, it means that certain factors such as race, religion, and sex cannot be used to bias outcomes.[24]

From a perspective of "a priori probabilities" in which people are not differentiated by race, religion, and sex (and, presumably, class) this strict definition should hold: "Equal opportunity means that, given some scarce indivisible good, X, and N persons wanting X, the probability that any person will get X, is $1/N$."[25]

Dorn argues that this rule, ambitious as it is, will not necessarily improve the overall position of blacks, even were it

24. Dorn, *Rules and Racial Equality*, p. 112.
25. Ibid.

to be fully instituted. Essentially, the argument comes down to this:

> Equal opportunity, if it existed, would mean that for every substantive gain whites make, blacks could be expected to make the same gain (relative to population, of course). If the races are unequal to begin with, that is, at the time when bias is eliminated, substantive inequality will persist.[26]

"The reason," Dorn explains, "is obvious: Equal opportunity applies only to marginal allocation."[27] Equal (per capita) marginal allocations when added to unequal starting points will produce unequal (per capita) results. Dorn's definition is not a "global" one applying to all goods, but a "marginal" one applying to additional increments.

Hence, the ideal of equal opportunity that has the disturbing implications identified in his argument is a less demanding ideal than the one we have identified as equal life chances. The "unequal starting points" presumed by Dorn's argument would not be accepted by an adequate ideal of equal opportunity. The transmission of inherited wealth, special advantages for the privileged, grossly unequal developmental conditions for the disadvantaged are all varieties of the unequal starting points that would undermine equal life chances. By contrast, the more demanding ideal of equal life chances applied globally regardless of such initial inequalities would not have the disturbing implication identified by Dorn, namely, the perpetuation of inequalities between races. As Dorn acknowledges later in his argument:

> Racial equality can be achieved under a rule of global equal opportunity. By global I mean that the rule applies to all goods, not just to a portion of future allocations.[28]

26. Ibid., p. 120.
27. Ibid., pp. 117–18.
28. Ibid., p. 139.

If goods are an appropriate value for assessing the positions in a principle of equal life chances, then this "global" principle is equivalent to equality of life chances. And full implementation of this principle would, over time, eliminate any systematic inequalities between groups.

Were equality of life chances to be fully implemented, it would offer an adequate response to the caste system problem. Unlike the less demanding marginal principle considered by Dorn, equality of life chances would define a version of equal opportunity that is not subject to the objection that it perpetuates existing inequalities between social groups, such as races (or ethnic groups).

Yet equality of life chances is an extremely demanding ideal and, perhaps, it might be argued, a preference for groups is an appropriate and effective remedy when the ideal of equal life chances is less than fully implemented. I believe, however, that a more careful examination of its implications would lead to the conclusion that it would not be an effective alternative to equal life chances in eliminating the lingering effects of a partially operative "caste" system, to use Fiss's term.

Recall Fiss's explicit inclusion of "rich blacks" in any program of preferential treatment. So long as the required benefits improve the position of blacks as a whole, it does not ultimately matter, according to such an aggregative group principle, how the benefits are distributed within the group. And, as we have seen, even proponents of such programs expect a substantial mistargeting of benefits to those who are not themselves extremely disadvantaged. In any competitive meritocratic context, it is the more advantaged minority group members who are likely to have the best qualifications—precisely because of the unequal developmental conditions that their more advantaged families are able to provide. Hence any program of preferential treatment applied to members of the group, as such, is likely to result in a substantial mistargeting of benefits.

While benefits to minority group members who are not,

themselves, extremely disadvantaged may serve laudable sym-
bolic purposes, they will not be effective in freeing the ghetto
underclass from a persisting caste system. To the extent that
the life chances of the truly disadvantaged are untouched by
such measures, the caste system will persist. On the other
hand, to the extent that preferential treatment is directed, not
to members of the group, as such, but, more specifically, to the
truly disadvantaged, in particular, the caste system will be
broken down. In other words, preferential treatment directed
specifically to disadvantaged individuals so as to improve
equality of life chances would constitute a more appropriate
remedy for a lingering caste system. As noted earlier, such
programs of preferential treatment would differ markedly from
any program of group preference, as such. Such particularized
programs would satisfy the requirement that each individual
benefited, be someone who was, himself, from a disadvantaged
background. In this way, by avoiding the mistargeting objection, such programs would require that, in exchange for any
sacrifice in merit, there be some improvement in equality of
life chances. These policies are compatible with our basic
framework of individualistic competition. They would not
require any introduction of a preference for a particular social
group, as such.

4.4 Unequal Positions

Thus far, I have considered a
variety of revisions in our ori-
ginal liberal formula that there should be a fair competition
among individuals for unequal positions in society. Some revisions focus on fairness, others on competition, and others on
the belief that competition should take place among individuals rather than among groups. Another revision in the formula that might avoid our trilemma would be to relax the
assumption of substantial background inequalities, both social
and economic. For then equal life chances would follow, trivi-
ally, from the mere fact of equal outcomes. The expected value

everyone would receive from the assignment process would be the same. Presumably, some matching of talents and qualifications with tasks to be performed still could be devised so as to conform to merit under such conditions. If so, then both components of equal opportunity could be implemented without any need to intervene in the family.

Our trilemma clearly could be avoided by such a move, but only at the cost of an even more radical requirement than the sacifice in family autonomy. Strict equalization of outcomes, both social and economic, were it possible at all, could be maintained in a modern industrialized society only at a substantial cost in liberty. One of this book's themes is that equal opportunity, like certain other process equalities at the core of modern liberalism, can only be achieved at a substantial cost in liberty. This cost in liberty may arise because of efforts to *insulate* social and economic inequalities from compromising the process equality (in this case, equal opportunity). Intervening intrusively in the family would constitute one form of insulation. Or, the cost in liberty may arise because of efforts to *eliminate* the social and economic inequalities directly. In either case, insulation or elimination, a substantial cost in liberty is unavoidable. I will pursue this more general argument in the next chapter.

It has long been a theme of libertarians that equality of outcomes could be maintained only at a substantial cost in liberty. It is more surprising, however, that even the apparently less drastic process principles of equal opportunity produce the same conflict. Once the role of the family is accounted for, the conflict between liberty and equality becomes an unavoidable problem at the core of liberal theory.

In order to cover all our alternatives, let us now examine why libertarians have long contended that strict equality could come only at a substantial cost in liberty. This will close off the only escape route for proponents of equal opportunity who might wish to avoid the conflicts with liberty directed at the family.

The issue is captured incisively and dramatically by Nozick's "Wilt Chamberlain" argument. We are asked to pick our
favorite "patterned" principle of justice and to imagine that a
distribution, D_1, has been realized that perfectly conforms to
it. Wilt Chamberlain, "a great gate attraction," signs a contract
giving him "twenty-five cents from the price of each ticket of
admission." After a million people attend the home games
(each dropping a quarter in boxes marked "Wilt"), Chamberlain "winds up with $250,000, a much larger sum than the
average income and larger even than anyone else has." Let us
call this new distribution D_2. Nozick's central claim is that:

> If D_1 was a just distribution and people voluntarily moved
> from it to D_2, transferring parts of their shares they were
> given under D_1 (what was it for if not to do something
> with?), isn't D_2 also just? If the people were entitled to
> dispose of the resources to which they were entitled (under
> D_1), didn't this include their being entitled to give it to, or
> exchange with, Wilt Chamberlain? Can anyone else com-
> plain on grounds of justice? Each other person already has
> his legitimate share under D_1. Under D_1, there is nothing
> that anyone else has a claim of justice against. After
> someone transfers something to Wilt Chamberlain, third
> parties still have their legitimate shares; *their* shares are
> unchanged.[29]

Nozick's general point is that any patterned principle, and in
particular, any egalitarian end-state principle, cannot be "con-
tinuously realized without continuous interference with people's lives."[30] Even a perfect pattern such as D_1 will be trans-
muted, through people simply exercising the property rights or
entitlements granted to them by the initially perfect distribution, into some *other* pattern, D_2, that may differ markedly
from the original one.

29. Nozick, *Anarchy, State, and Utopia*, p. 161.
30. Ibid., p. 163.

We need not follow Nozick in his overly strong conclusion that D_2 must be as just as D_1, in order to realize that he is correct in the basic claim that "liberty upsets patterns."[31] People merely exercising the entitlements granted to them by some initial distribution will produce varying alternative distributions. It must be emphasized, however, that restrictions on this liberty to exercise entitlements may lead to greater justice according to some structural or patterned principle of justice.[32] Whether these latter conceptions are more or less adequate than the bare entitlement conception cannot be settled here.[33] For Nozick to reach the conclusion that D_2 must be "as just" as D_1, he would have to *assume* that the voluntary exercise of entitlements must be *sufficient* to settle the question of the justice of a distribution. He must, in other words, simply assume a particular and controversial answer to the very problem at issue in the example.

While justice, in some sense that takes account of structural or patterned considerations, may require a sacrifice in the liberty of people to exercise their entitlements, it is important to realize that the required sacrifice in liberty is a real one. Nozick's argument dramatizes how the liberties of property, contract, and employment (included in his entitlement conception of rights distributed in D_1), if left unfettered by other moral constraints, will overturn initially just patterns, especially egalitarian ones. As Nozick concludes:

> To maintain a pattern one must either continually interfere to stop people from transferring resources as they wish to, or continually (or periodically) interfere to take from some persons resources that others for some reason chose to transfer to them.[34]

31. Ibid., p. 160.

32. "Patterned" principles include all end-state principles (the latter term applies to principles such as equality or utilitarianism answering the structural problem we discussed in section 2.2). See Nozick, *Anarchy, State, and Utopia,* p. 156.

33. See my critique of the bare entitlement conception in *Tyranny and Legitimacy,* chapter 9.

34. Nozick, *Anarchy, State, and Utopia,* p. 163.

This argument applies to "any distributional pattern with an egalitarian component" and to any other distributional principles "with sufficient content so as actually to have been proposed as presenting the central core of distributive justice."[35]

While maintenance of any egalitarian distributional pattern would require continuous coercive interference, it should be obvious that maintenance of strict equality would require even more continuous and extreme interference than would most alternative principles. Any consensual bargain between two or more persons or groups that yields a departure from equal shares for anyone would require prohibition or subsequent redistribution undoing the effects of the bargain or contract. Systematic suppression of liberties of property, contract, and employment (so far as the latter involves any reference to wages or benefits) would be required. The more closely a principle attempted to maintain strict equality, the more systematic would this coercive interference and oversight have to be.

Of course, liberties of property, contract, and employment sometimes benefit the more advantaged far more than anyone else. Yet this protection of privilege is not in any way essential to the argument. One of the more interesting aspects of Nozick's example is that it dramatizes how these liberties would have to be suppressed, even if the pattern to be maintained were one of perfect equality. In fact, the example works most clearly if perfect equality is the principle under D_1; then it is clear that voluntary transactions between consenting groups or individuals will serve, over time, to upset the pattern. Furthermore, none of these voluntary acts need produce any harm to third parties. Hence, these consensual relations can be viewed as falling under a negative liberty claim, protected by the harm principle (see section 2.4). Nozick's theory can be viewed as protecting "capitalist acts between consenting adults." Maintaining equality over time would require the

35. Ibid., p. 164.

continuous suppression of such capitalist acts (of exchange, contract, and employment), as these might be carried out by consenting adults without harm to third parties.[36] It is in this sense that realizing equality of outcomes would require a systematic and substantial sacrifice of liberty.

Of course even the principle of merit might be held to involve a sacrifice of liberty in some sense. For example, conservatives have sometimes attacked formal notions of equal opportunity as an interference with the liberty of potential employees and employers to make whatever bargains they like. I do not deny that the equality claim in the principle of merit (a procedural claim to equal consideration of one's qualifications) involves some sacrifice in a recognizable form of liberty. Every other form of equality discussed in this book also involves a sacrifice in liberty.

While the liberty sacrificed by merit takes a recognizable form, it can be distinguished from the sphere of negative liberty I have been employing that protects consensual acts that do not harm third parties. The issue depends upon what benchmark is accepted for assessing harm to third parties.

It is arguable that if people earn qualifications according to publicly acknowledged practices of meritocratic assignment, then they have acquired conditional entitlements; they merit certain results depending on how their qualifications would be evaluated in a fair competition. To depart from a fair competition and discriminate against persons arbitrarily is, in the context of such meritocratic practices, to impose a harm on those who have gone to the trouble to earn the qualifications. It is to impose a harm on those who would have been assigned

36. Nozick often relies on an analogy between consensual, intimate acts and consensual property relations. His rhetorical strategy is often to extend the protection liberals customarily provide to the former, to the latter as well. See his comparison of distribution problems to the choice of mates in *Anarchy, State, and Utopia*, pp. 150, 167, and 237. I believe that this kind of extension must face the issue of benchmarks for assessing harm and the problem of omissions in the causation of harm. I discuss the former in the paragraphs on meritocracy in the text following this citation. See my discussion of the latter in *Tyranny and Legitimacy*, chapter 9.

to the positions, had there been a fair competition conducted according to publicly acknowledged practices. If we accept this benchmark defined by meritocratic practices for the assessment of harm, then arbitrary or discriminatory employment contracts departing from merit do harm third parties. In that case they do not fall within the protected sphere of negative liberty defined by the harm principle.

The main issue, in this section, however, is whether equality of outcomes, rather than equality of opportunities, would require a substantial sacrifice in liberty. Libertarians such as Hayek and Nozick[37] have always argued that this must be the case. It is worth pausing, however, to consider a novel counterargument to this claim, offered by Joseph Carens in a recent book.[38] Carens constructs a hypothetical scenario for realizing strict equality of income without, he argues, any substantial cost in either efficiency or liberty. In an admittedly "utopian" argument, he bids us to envision an imaginary egalitarian society that conforms precisely to a private-property-market (or PPM) system except for these essential modifications:

> First, individuals in the second system [his proposal] believe they have a social duty to earn as much pre-tax net income as they are capable of earning.
>
> Second, individuals in the second system derive satisfaction from performing this social duty to earn as much pretax income as they can.
>
> Third, individuals in the second system place the same relative value on the satisfaction derived from performing their social duty to acquire pre-tax income (hereafter called social duty satisfaction) as individuals in the first system (the PPM system) place on the satisfactions derived from acquiring income for consumption (hereafter called income-consumption satisfaction).[39]

37. See chapter 1, n. 4.
38. Carens, *Equality, Moral Incentives, and the Market.*
39. Ibid., p. 25.

Among the additional "logical" prerequisites for the argument, the most important is the requirement that the tax laws provide a perfectly equal after-tax income distribution without any significant loopholes and that these tax laws be generally obeyed.[40]

Carens makes the case, with considerable clarity and detail, that if individuals were successfully socialized so as to acquire the preferences specified in the three conditions cited above, the politico-economic system could be expected to function successfully without any loss of efficiency, as compared to an otherwise identical, private-property-market system employing substantial inequalities as incentives. I will not dispute the efficiency claim Carens makes for these admittedly utopian, if not implausible, conditions. Despite a few complications, it is fairly clear that *if* individuals in a hypothetical, egalitarian system placed exactly the same value on the "social duty satisfaction" to maximize pre-tax income that they now place on "income-consumption satisfactions," then such a system could operate rather like our present system.[41] If their preferences really were structured in that way, then their efforts and motivations would not be undermined in the least by the fact that confiscatory marginal income tax rates were designed to leave them all with precisely the same after-tax incomes. There would, in other words, be no loss of efficiency because of lost incentive effects in a society composed largely of individuals who held such preferences.

More central to our topic here, however, is Carens's claim that his system could also be realized without any great cost in *liberty* compared to the freedom available in a more conventional private-property-market system. This latter claim is defended in two steps: the first concerns freedom of employ-

40. See Carens's list of prerequisites, ibid., pp. 174–76.
41. An issue might, however, be raised about demand. Carens assumes demand will be the same in the two systems, but it will surely be affected by the much more limited after-tax income available to consumers under his proposal. See pp. 24–25.

ment and consumption; the second concerns the conditions for preference formation. Let us begin with Carens's claim that his system would maintain "freedom of choice in occupation" and "freedom of choice in consumption."[42] Under Carens's egalitarian plan people can enter the job market and pursue careers in exactly the way they do in a PPM system—with the one proviso that no matter what they do, they cannot keep any more or less than the equal income they would have received anyway. Similarly, they can spend their income on consumer goods precisely as they do now—with the one proviso that no matter what they do, they cannot spend more than their alloted equal income share.

While there is a sense in which freedom of choice of both occupation and consumption is preserved, we have only to return to Nozick's Wilt Chamberlain example to see how freedom of property, contract, and employment are actually restricted by Carens's system. True, Wilt Chamberlain could still enter the market for basketball players, he could still negotiate a hefty contract for pre-tax income (if he happened to share the preference for maximizing "social duty satisfaction" in Carens's sense), and lastly, 1,000,000 spectators could still place their quarters in boxes marked "Wilt." The one difference is that Chamberlain could not keep *any* of the proceeds (above the equal income allotment he would receive anyway, were he not to play a single game). All one million quarters and any other income from his hefty contract would have to be given over to the government. It is undeniable that a central liberty connected to employment and consumption has been lost: the *liberty to engage in consensual market relations so as to affect one's material well-being and, in particular, so as to affect one's after-tax income.*

The spectators, presumably, are placing the quarters in boxes marked "Wilt" in order to give the quarters to Chamberlain, not in order to give the quarters to the government. Chamber-

42. Ibid., pp. 90–91.

lain, presumably, negotiates a contract and plays professional basketball in order to earn a salary for himself, not in order to add to aggregate government revenues. It is the liberty to pursue acts that accomplish these objectives—purposes that impose no harm on third parties—that must be thwarted by Carens's system. Liberty of employment cannot remain unaffected by programs that destroy the ability of employees to have any effect whatsoever on their material well-being. The wage bargain, and its connection to after-tax income, is an intrinsic part of liberty of employment. Programs that would completely suppress wage bargains—so far as they might affect after-tax income in any way—must be considered a drastic curtailment of liberty of employment.

Of course, income taxation is a familiar part of most private-property-market systems. But income taxation at any of the familiar marginal rates raises different issues from those raised by 100 percent confiscatory taxation for any marginal increments above strict equality. Such a system would render it impossible for persons to have any effect on their levels of material well-being (after-tax income) by engaging in market relations. To the extent that consensual market relations between persons or groups do not harm others, they can be viewed as protected by the sphere of negative liberty discussed earlier. Because Carens's system must thwart every possible act of contract, gift, employment, or exchange intended to affect after-tax income, the proposal would require systematic coercive interferences banning, to use the phrase employed earlier, all "capitalist acts between consenting adults" so far as they are aimed at affecting the income of any of the participants.

In addition to this sacrifice in the liberties of property, contract, and employment, another disturbing possibility must be faced squarely. The only known experiments with "moral incentives" as replacements for (after-tax) income incentives have required "preceptoral education"—systematic efforts at indoctrination and thought control.[43] Carens attempts to dismiss such indoctrination by accepting it as a requirement for transition but not necessarily as a requirement for maintenance once the egalitarian system was fully in place. He denies "that the socialization process would have to be consciously planned and managed by a highly centralized bureaucracy."[44] Even though the socialization process that produced uniformly high preferences for social duty satisfaction would have to be "more intense" than the socialization process in a PPM system:

> The point is that it is quite possible to have a highly intensive socialization process which attaches great social importance to some particular goal and yet which is decentralized, informal, and even, for many of the agents of socialization, unconscious and unintended.[45]

Just as our present emphasis on socializing income incentives is decentralized and not consciously coordinated, Carens believes that it might be possible for an egalitarian system, once established, to leave the process of passing on norms of social duty satisfaction to the same decentralized process.

I believe, however, that there are reasons to be quite skeptical that such a system could maintain itself without continued and severe restrictions on the process of preference formation. For Carens's argument to work, social duty satisfaction must have the same widespread acceptance and relevance for behavior that the desire for income has in more conventional market systems. Families, schools, peer groups, advertisers, the electronic and print media, the example of opinion leaders would all have to be marshalled for—or at least, prevented from undermining—the required socialization process aimed at pro-

43. See Lindblom, *Politics and Markets,* chapters 4 and 21; and Bernardo, *The Theory of Moral Incentives in Cuba.*
44. Carens, *Equality, Moral Incentives, and the Market,* p. 119.
45. Ibid.

ducing persons who believe they have a social duty to earn as much pre-tax income as possible. It is doubtful whether the required uniformity and centrality for this particular normative preference could arise throughout the society without a campaign of indoctrination and manipulation.

Note, for example, that without restrictions on liberty, the very market system Carens hopes to maintain with his equal income proposal would be the source of major disruptive influences to the required socialization. Corporations in the hypothesized large-scale market economy would have the same incentives, that they have now in more conventional market systems, to advertise and to do whatever they possibly can to stimulate demand for their products. The pervasive influence of advertising on preference development should not be underestimated.[46] Unless there were restrictions on liberty of expression, advertising, a major and systematic component of the socialization process, would influence individuals to maximize consumption of an enormous variety of consumer goods. These familiar pressures would surely undermine compliance with a social duty norm to consume only a precisely equal share and hand over the rest to the government. The already well-known compliance problems for major income tax systems would be dwarfed by those faced by a confiscatory 100 percent tax—particularly if it were not bolstered by concerted efforts at indoctrination.

It is also worth noting that if a system of free expression were in place, one could reasonably expect a diversity of values, religions, and creeds to flourish. Indeed, one might even carry the argument further and claim that without that diversity, freedom of opinion and freedom of conscience would, in an important sense, be fundamentally undermined. Unless people are exposed to a sufficient variety of alternatives, socialization becomes indoctrination and people lose any autonomy they might otherwise have had in developing their

46. See Lindblom, *Politics and Markets,* chapter 16.

opinions.[47] If this extension of the argument were accepted, then a diversity of creeds, values, religions, and other viewpoints on important moral and political questions would, itself, be a precondition for meaningful freedom of opinion and of conscience. But such a diversity of creeds, values, religions, and political opinions would hardly be compatible with Carens's hypothesis. For his argument would require homogeneous, intense, and nearly universal agreement on a particular and controversial construction of everyone's "social duty." If other moral, political, and religious opinions were sufficiently diverse, could one really expect such an extraordinary convergence on a particular normative issue to be maintained without coordinated efforts at indoctrination? And such campaigns of indoctrination and preference manipulation would, of course, constitute an important part of the price in liberty necessary for such a system.[48]

Convergence on a particular normative issue, such as the "social duty" preference required for moral incentives, should be distinguished from the actual convergence of preferences found in conventional market systems on the value of *after*-tax income. As Rawls notes, income is a "primary good"; it is an instrumental value that is likely to be of great use in any market system, whatever one's particular theory of the good and whatever one's particular normative perspective.[49] While there are a few notable exceptions, such as asceticism, even adherents to such positions may find a use for money in proselytizing or protecting their cherished beliefs. This instrumental character of money, regardless of one's particular val-

47. See Mill, *On Liberty*, chapters 2 and 3. For a recent systematic argument for a similar conclusion, see Ackerman, *Social Justice*, especially chapters 5, 10, and 11.
48. See section 5.1 for the role of this sacrifice in liberty in the more general argument.
49. Rawls, *Theory of Justice*, pp. 90–95. This general point can be accepted without the more particular assumptions about primary goods necessary for Rawls's argument. See my "Justice and Rationality" for a critique of these latter assumptions.

ues or creed, thus should be distinguished from the kind of normative consensus that would be required to systematically socialize all members of society into agreement on a particular normative issue with more substantive content, in other words, that everyone has a "social duty" to maximize pre-tax income, all additional increments of which ought to be given to the government.

It might be objected that the need just identified for a sacrifice in liberty only arises if the system attempts to maintain perfect equality without any cost in efficiency. Suppose, however, that we were to abandon attempts at indoctrination and accept the resulting sacrifice in efficiency. The costs in liberty of property, contract, and employment would still arise. Furthermore, the widespread lack of compliance that would result from lack of acceptance of the required social duty norm could be expected to increase the need for coercive interference to enforce compliance so far as possible. Would people work at all if they were guaranteed an equal income and were not indoctrinated to consider their contribution a social duty? In any case, a great deal of coercion and surveillance would be required to guarantee compliance with the confiscatory income tax (for all increments above strict equality) and to prevent black markets, underground economies, barter, and the other strategies that could be expected to flourish if the required social duty norms were not widely accepted and deeply entrenched.

The sacrifice in liberty required by Carens's scenario illustrates one side of a more general dilemma. Inequalities can only be eliminated at a substantial cost in liberty. Although I have focused on economic inequalities, any thorough effort to eliminate background inequalities would have to confront *social* inequalities as well. It has been speculated that the division of labor and the enforcement of norms required for a complex modern society render social inequalities fundamentally ineradicable. I will not enter this controversy here but will only pause to note that the egalitarian strategy of avoiding difficulties in equal opportunity through the implementation of equal results would confront, at some point, the challenge that anything approaching social equality may not be possible in a complex industrial society.[50] I would speculate, however, that given a substantial sacrifice in liberty, it might prove possible, no matter what the division of labor. With sufficient thought control, a strictly egalitarian ethos might be maintained, no matter what the differentiation of skills and roles. Of course, such thought control would only increase the required sacrifice in liberty.

Either a substantial sacrifice in liberty or a substantial sacrifice in equal opportunity must be accepted. Stated simply, this is the general problem underlying our discussion of equal opportunity. In constructing the trilemma, I assumed the application of background inequalities; if the door is opened to efforts at eliminating (and maintaining the elimination of) these economic and social inequalities, then a sacrifice in liberty of a different kind results from any serious effort to avoid the trilemma.

Given background inequalities, we must choose between the strong doctrine of equal opportunity (merit and equal life chances) and the autonomy of the family. To sacrifice either component of the former would seriously compromise equal opportunity, as we have seen. To sacrifice the latter would represent a disturbing cost in the sphere of liberty most precious to the way most of us live. The only remaining alternative is to relax the assumption of background inequalities with a resultant cost in liberty of a different kind. We must choose between equal opportunity, on the one hand, and liberty, on the other. In the latter case, the liberties are admittedly heterogeneous—the private sphere involved in the family can be distinguished from the liberties of property, contract, and employment at issue in the equalization strategy. Despite the different spheres of application, these liberties can all be

50. See chapter 3, nn. 11 and 12.

thought of as applying to consensual acts that do not directly and significantly harm third parties. In that sense they can all be subsumed within the broader framework of negative liberty defined by the harm principle.

The general point is that the conflict between liberty and equality arises dramatically even when the equality principle falls short of demanding equal results and requires only equal opportunities to be unequal. Once the family is taken into account, as I have tried to do here, the general conflict comes into clear focus. Equal opportunity, if taken seriously, is a radical notion with far reaching implications. Even under the simplifying conditions of ideal theory, its conflict with liberty is unavoidable. If liberal theory is to offer us a coherent and defensible ideal, then we must face squarely the conflicts that were obscured heretofore by our blindness to the role of the family. If we want more equal opportunity, we must be willing to undergo some sacrifice in liberty. If we want to preserve liberty, we must be willing to sacrifice, or significantly compromise, equal opportunity. If we blithely advocate the full realization of both sides in this forced choice, then we are failing to offer a defensible ideal that might coherently guide public policy under realistic conditions.

4.5 Policy Implications   This book has focused on a question of ideal theory. Given background conditions of inequality what would be the implications, even under ideal conditions, of attempting to institute a fair competition among individuals for assignment to social positions? As I have shown, the implications are quite radical. We must either sacrifice the autonomy of the family or we must achieve equality of results. Either of these latter options would require a substantial sacrifice in liberty. On the other hand, to avoid the sacrifice in liberty, we must seriously compromise one or the other component of our doctrine of equal opportunity. This conjunction of liberal commitments produces a series of disturbing scenarios even under ideal conditions (that is, even when strict compliance and only moderate scarcity apply).

However, we do not directly face the problems of ideal theory in actual public policy. This pattern of conflicting principles only means that once the role of the family is realistically taken into account common liberal commitments do not add up to a unified and coherent ideal.

In actual public policy, however, we are very far from facing these trade-offs of ideal theory. Each of the principles cited, while often invoked in policy debates, is only imperfectly implemented. We do not have now a meritocratic system of assignment. We do not have now substantial equality of life chances. And family autonomy is now far more a reality for middle income and rich families than it is for poor ones.[51] We could better realize each of these three principles without producing any further requirement to sacrifice one of the others. There is much that could be done to root out the lingering racial and ethnic discrimination that undermines merit. And there is much that could be done to endow poor people with the same protection for family autonomy granted to other strata.

Most dramatically, there is a great deal that might be done to increase equality of life chances without requiring any sacrifice in either merit or family autonomy. We need to continue, indeed to expand, the Great Society's wave of social experimentation with efforts to improve the developmental conditions of the least advantaged.[52] Such efforts may not, as I

51. See Justice Blackmun's eloquent dissent in the recent case Lassiter v. Dept. of Social Services of Durham County, North Carolina 452 U.S. 18 (1980). Blackmun defends the right of indigent parents to state-paid legal assistance in child custody cases. Otherwise, they may be virtually defenseless in confronting efforts by state agencies to take away their children.
52. See Sar A. Levitan and Robert Taggart, III, *The Promise of Greatness* (Cambridge: Harvard University Press, 1976); and Edward Zigler and Jeannette Valentine, eds., *Project Head Start: A Legacy of the War on Poverty* (New York: Free Press, 1981). See also the home-based strategies referred to here in chapter 3, n. 58.

argued in chapter three, *equalize* life chances regardless of social class or family background. Nevertheless, there are many government interventions, compatible with both family autonomy and merit in assignment, that may lead to far greater equality of life chances than has been achieved thus far. Year after year, black teenage unemployment has hovered around 40 percent in many of our nation's cities.[53] The life chances of a whole generation have been blighted by inadequate opportunities to acquire skills and jobs. We need to think more creatively and to act more resolutely in implementing strategies of intervention directed at the home environment, schools, peer groups, and all local institutions having a direct impact on child development. Youth employment opportunities, on-the-job training, and nontraditional forms of education all need greatly expanded funding and more creative experimentation.

Even our relatively successful programs have received lackluster support. Gerald Gill noted in 1980 about Head Start, that despite its considerable growth:

A majority of children eligible for participation in Head Start programs still do not have the opportunity because of inadequate funds. Because of inadequate funding, not as many children as are eligible take advantage of Title I programs. It has been estimated that in New York City alone there are 151,000 pupils who are eligible for Title I programs but do not participate.[54]

Recent cuts by the Reagan administration in food stamps, school lunch programs, Medicaid, and a host of other services are likely to affect directly the physical and economic wellbeing of children in poor families.

In all of these cases, there are obvious opportunities to target policies so as to improve the life chances of children born into

53. See "The American Underclass," *Time* 110 (August 29, 1977), and Andrew Brimmer, "Youth in the Labor Market," *Black Enterprise* (May 1981), p. 59.
54. Gerald R. Gill, *Meanness Mania: The Changed Mood* (Washington, D.C.: Howard University Press, 1980) p. 22.

disadvantaged families. Such interventions may improve, rather than undermine, the integrity of those families (without affecting family autonomy in other strata). Furthermore, such policies need raise no conflict with the principles of merit employed for adult assignment. When realization of one of our core principles can be furthered without any corresponding sacrifice in one of the others, there is an obvious case for the effort. The case is more controversial when one principle must be sacrificed in order to realize another. My point is that the easy, less controversial case is available to justify a host of policies that might improve equality of life chances in our present social context.

The other obvious policy implication is one I have discussed already in some detail. Just as there is an easy case for improvements in one principle that do not require sacrifices in another, there is also an easy case against sacrifices in one principle that do not bring improvements in another. Recall my earlier argument against policies of preferential treatment merely according to group characteristics such as race or ethnic origin. Unless the particular empirical context makes it reasonable to suppose that such policies will be targeted primarily towards persons who are themselves disadvantaged, such policies run the risk of dramatically sacrificing merit without any corresponding improvement in equality of life chances.

Ironically, while the program that the court refused to rule on in *DeFunis* was subject to this obvious objection, the quite different program of preferential treatment that the court struck down in *Bakke*, whatever its other defects, was unusual in being targeted toward disadvantaged blacks. As Sindler notes about the special admission program at the University of California at Davis: "the Davis program, unlike most others, did not call for giving preference to solidly middle-class minority applicants over lower-class whites" (or whites of any other background).[55] Each application was searched "for such clues as whether he has been granted a waiver of the application fee,

55. Sindler, *Bakke, DeFunis, and Minority Admissions*, pp. 57–58.

which requires a means test, whether he had in the past participated in programs for the disadvantaged, whether he worked during school, and the occupational background and education of his parents."[56] While there is some controversy about how this search was administered, there appears to have been a clear effort to target preferential treatment toward persons who were, themselves, disadvantaged.[57] Whatever the other defects in the Davis program, it is thus arguable that it fulfilled our minimum conditions. The cost in merit was, at least, accompanied by a policy that would improve equality of life chances. From this perspective, the court's solution was regrettable. For it struck down a program targeted toward persons who were actually disadvantaged while it encouraged the explicit consideration of race as a qualification, in itself, under the banner of "diversity."

As we have seen, such straightforward racial preferences are subject to the mistargeting objection. For that reason they are vulnerable to the charge that they sacrifice one of our principles without producing any gain in the others. Furthermore, compensatory arguments for past injustice lead to a similar focus on the disadvantaged (rather than on race per se) when those compensatory arguments are applied to individuals rather than to groups. And, as we saw above, it is only the individualistic version of such arguments that seems defensible. Thus within the framework developed here, current public policies are vulnerable to some obvious criticisms, both because of the severe injustices that are blindly tolerated (the inequality in life chances and developmental conditions that might be lessened) and because of the remedies that seem misdirected (preferences for racial or ethnic groups per se). Even without an ideal solution to the general theoretical

56. Bakke v. Regents of University of California, 553 p.2d 1152, at 1158, n. 8.

57. There is some controversy about the extent to which this policy was actually applied. See the Brief of the American Jewish Committee as amicus curiae, *Bakke*, p. 51, n. 26.

problem we can argue, nevertheless, that there is much that should be transformed in the current American policies aimed at equal opportunity.

5. OPTIONS FOR
LIBERAL THEORY

*5.1 Contemporary Lib-
eralism: The General Issue* The ingredients for the trilemma of equal opportunity
are a familiar part of American public ideology and political
theory. It is worth pausing for a moment to consider two
preeminent examples—Lyndon B. Johnson's famous speech at
Howard University in support of his Great Society program
and John Rawls's systematic expression of liberalism in *A
Theory of Justice*. I pick these two examples from many
possibilities because Johnson's Great Society was the most
important policy initiative in modern American history aimed
at improving the developmental conditions necessary for equal
opportunity. And Rawls's book is clearly the most influential
work of liberal political theory to appear recently in America.

Johnson employed the central metaphor of a footrace, a race
that not only must be procedurally fair, but that also must
realize background fairness in the conditions for acquiring the
abilities measured in the race:

> You do not take a person who, for years, has been hobbled
> by chains and liberate him, bring him up to the starting
> line of a race and then say, "you are free to compete with
> all the others," and still justly believe that you have been
> completely fair.[1]

Applying this metaphor to America's "20 million Negroes,"
the task is to give them:

1. *Public Papers of the Presidents of the United States, Lyndon B. Johnson:
Containing the Public Messages, Speeches and Statements of the President
1965* (Washington, D.C.: Government Printing Office, 1966), p. 636.

The same chance as every other American to learn and grow, to work and share in society, to develop their abilities—physical, mental and spiritual, and to pursue their individual happiness.[2]

Johnson acknowledged that this equalization of developmental conditions in training for the race, giving blacks "the same chance . . . to develop their abilities," would require a transformation of a host of environmental factors. These include the family:

Ability is not just the product of birth. Ability is stretched or stunted by the family that you live with, and the neighborhood you live in—by the school you go to and the poverty or richness of your surroundings. It is the product of a hundred unseen forces playing upon the little infant, the child, and finally the man.[3]

And among these forces, the family is crucial: "The family is the cornerstone of our society. More than any other force it shapes the attitudes, the hopes, the ambitions and the values of the child."[4]

Johnson's historic speech contains all the elements necessary for constructing our trilemma. To maintain what we have been calling merit is simply to enforce the rules of competition in the "race." To equalize chances to develop abilities for the competition would be to equalize life chances for outcomes determined by the race. But to do so would require manipulation of the "hundred unseen forces," including the family, that shape the development of abilities.

Of course, Johnson's purpose was not to construct a general theory of equal opportunity for ideal conditions. Rather, it was to find a direction for policies that might soon affect the crisis conditions actually applying. Surely in this latter goal he set a

2. Ibid.
3. Ibid.
4. Ibid., p. 639.

standard for presidential speeches that has not often been equaled. And in formulating this direction, surely he was wise to focus on immediate strategies for leveling up, strategies that might improve the nutrition, health care, and preschool education of the worst-off. The theoretical questions I have raised—how such strategies must fall short of *equalizing* developmental conditions and of giving every American, black or white, rich or poor, "the same chance as every other American to learn and grow ... to develop their abilities"—would have seemed irrelevant philosophical issues at the time. There was too much immediate progress to be made to worry about how we might eventually fall short of some ideal.

Yet it is worth emphasizing that this philosophical issue, central for our purposes, arises simply from any effort to take seriously common commitments that are an acknowledged part of American public ideology. We cannot maintain these simultaneous commitments with any pretense that together they identify a coherent direction for public policy without also confronting the hard choices explored in the last two chapters. Under any realistic construction of the options available, even under ideal conditions, they cannot all be realized simultaneously. We must either abandon one or more of these commitments, or we must modify them by admitting their susceptibility to sacrifice—by admitting that they can be traded-off one for another or sacrificed according to certain priority relations. The important point is that, given any remotely realistic construction of the empirical possibilities, to require *simultaneous* realization of all these commitments would be to advocate an incoherent ideal for public policy.

Just such a charge plausibly can be directed at John Rawls's doctrine of fair equality of opportunity, when it is combined with his comments about the family. Rawls's principle of fair equality of opportunity includes the principle of merit as we have been conceiving it, the requirement of what he calls "careers open to talents." But it goes much farther, approximating equality of life chances in his formula that: "Positions are to be not only open in a formal sense, but all should have a fair chance to attain them."[5] In part this means that "those with similar abilities and skills should have similar life chances."[6] The issue turns, of course, on the conditions for developing abilities and skills. On this issue, he arrives at a formula for equalizing life chances regardless of income classes, for giving equal prospects to those who do similarly well in the lottery of natural assets:

> More specifically, assuming that there is a distribution of natural assets, those who are at the same level of talent and ability, and have the same willingness to use them, should have the same prospects of success regardless of their initial place in the social system, that is, irrespective of the income class into which they are born.[7]

Rawls's formula yields equality of life chances regardless of income class provided that there are equal chances in all strata to develop skills and motivations. Rawls takes this step as a matter of principle but then shrinks from applying it to the family:

> *Chances to acquire cultural knowledge and skills should not depend upon one's class position,* and so the school system, whether public or private, should be designed to even out class barriers [emphasis added].[8]

Rawls admits, however, that school systems are likely to be ineffective by themselves at equalizing developmental conditions, regardless of class barriers. Because of the crucial role of the family, Rawls therefore concludes that his principle "can be only imperfectly carried out":

> The principle of fair opportunity *can be only imperfectly carried out, at least so long as the institution of the family exists.* The extent to which natural capacities develop and

5. Rawls, *Theory of Justice*, p. 73.
6. Ibid.
7. Ibid.
8. Ibid.

reach fruition is affected by all kinds of social conditions and class attitudes. Even the willingness to make an effort, to try and so to be deserving in the ordinary sense is itself dependent upon happy family and social circumstances [emphasis added].[9]

Here is an explicit acknowledgement of the conflict between the family as we know it and the equalization of developmental conditions that would be required for equal life chances once merit (or "careers open to talents") is assumed. Rawls's strategy of "adding" to careers open to talents a "fair chance to attain" the positions allocated by merit leads him down essentially the same road toward equal developmental conditions that we travelled in chapters two and three above. He stops short of intruding upon the family, however, and concludes instead that his principle can be "only imperfectly carried out." It is unclear why fair equality of opportunity, a principle that has lexical priority over all other principles except liberty, is to be left imperfectly realized because of the family.[10] Perhaps Rawls would accept an argument like the one offered here that protecting the family should be interpreted as a matter of liberty, and hence, should fall under a principle of comparable, if not greater, priority.

As there is no hint of such an argument in the book, there is no need for us to speculate here on reformulations of Rawls's theory. We only need note that by permitting the family to stand as a barrier against the full realization of fair equality of opportunity, Rawls is endowing the remaining element of our trilemma with an independent normative status. He is granting the family sufficient weight to withstand the pressure of fair equality of opportunity, that is, to prevent its full realization.

As noted before, Rawls commits himself clearly to merit since "careers open to talents" is an explicit part of his fair opportunity principle. And since he states that "chances to

9. Ibid., p. 74.
10. Ibid., sections 8 and 11.

acquire cultural knowledge and skill should not depend upon one's class position," and that "those with similar abilities and skills should have similar life chances," something approaching equality of life chances regardless of class position is clearly his aim.

Yet as Rawls acknowledges, the logic of this position leads directly to conflicts with the family. It is mystifying why a principle that must be fully realized before other components of the theory of justice can come into place, must also remain forever imperfectly realized "in practice" because of conflicts with the family. Since fair equality of opportunity is treated elsewhere as a principle that can and must be fully realized, one can only conclude that the conflicts embodied in the trilemma have not been faced squarely. By aspiring to approximate both equal life chances and merit (with background inequalities applying),[11] while also granting the normative appropriateness of leaving the family unaffected, Rawls grants all the conditions necessary for our trilemma without venturing to offer a solution. We simply cannot realistically expect to realize merit, approximate equal life chances and, at the same time, leave the family unaffected, given the background conditions of inequality that Rawls also grants. By simultaneously affirming all of these commitments, Rawls has failed to offer us a coherent scenario for "fair equality of opportunity," even under the ideal conditions presumed by the argument.

I cite both Rawls's book and Johnson's speech only to show

11. Maximin should not be confused with equality. Depending on the operation of incentive effects, it may greatly increase inequality, provided that benefits to the worst-off are accompanied by sufficiently great benefits to other strata. While Rawls hopes that the institutionalization of fair equality of opportunity will, itself, tend to limit inequalities, this empirical tendency (if it were to apply) would surely not produce equalization to the point of undermining our assumption that there are background inequalities. For a discussion of the substantial inequalities that Rawls's theory would legitimate see Brian Barry, *The Liberal Theory of Justice* (Oxford: Clarendon Press, 1973), p. 156. A crucial factor is Rawls's explicit provision that the liberty principle does not require equalization of income and wealth. One may have equal liberty despite the unequal "worth" of liberty. See Norman Daniels, "Equal Liberty and Unequal Worth of Liberty," in Daniels, ed., *Reading Rawls*.

how the best of recent American public ideology has been committed to the ingredients required for our trilemma. My point, of course, is not to discredit liberal theory but only to emphasize that a more adequate version of liberalism must face certain hard choices that have, heretofore, been glossed over. This book is an effort to chart the terrain for such a reformulation.

I believe, however, that the equal opportunity problem I have explored here is far from unique. It is but a specific version of a more general issue facing liberalism. The essential core of contemporary liberalism can be thought of as a series of process equalities—institutionalized practices designed to guarantee equal consideration of everyone's preferences or interests. The doctrine of equal opportunity explored here is but one process equality; both in public debate and in theoretical work, liberals commonly advocate others that are equally essential. Political equality, equality before the law and, more controversially, equality of consideration for one's interests by the health care system offer good examples. I agree with other recent theorists—Rawls, Dworkin, Walzer, and Ackerman among others—who identify this notion of equal concern and respect for everyone as the "nerve" of liberalism.[12] And the most essential part of this doctrine, in both theory and practice, has been the notion that this equal concern and respect should be *institutionalized* in certain publicly sanctioned practices that affect especially important areas of life.

12. The original position is, of course, a way of formalizing equal concern and respect for everyone. For general comments on liberalism, see Ronald Dworkin, "Liberalism" in Stuart Hampshire, ed., *Public and Private Morality* (Cambridge: Cambridge University Press, 1978), pp. 113–43. In particular, see his comment on p. 115: "a certain conception of equality, is the nerve of liberalism." Ackerman's conception of "neutrality" in his *Social Justice* rests on a similar interpretation of liberalism. Also see Michael Walzer's defense of equality, centrally concerned with "the abolition of the power of money outside its sphere." This concern is "liberal" in the sense developed here (see my discussion of process equalities), although Walzer would term it "democratic socialist" (a position I would wish to include within liberalism in any case). See Michael Walzer, *Radical Principles: Reflections of an Unreconstructed Democrat* (New York: Basic Books, 1980), p. 240.

The same fundamental issue we confronted in the trilemma of equal opportunity recurs for the other process equalities just mentioned. Because these process equalities cover only certain specially designated spheres of life, they coexist, in modern complex industrial societies, with background inequalities, both social and economic, of the sort we presumed in our equal opportunity argument. The difficulty is that these background inequalities spill over, in each case, so as to undermine the process equality. Just as advantaged strata receive more than equal developmental conditions thereby undermining equal opportunity, they also easily obtain more than equal political influence (both direct and indirect), and more than equal consideration of their interests from the legal and health care systems. In each case, this spill-over effect undermines a process equality that has been held to be at the core of a defensible liberalism.

The parallel can be stated more precisely. Recall that our trilemma arose from a forced choice among three qualitatively distinct kinds of considerations: (a) the *procedural fairness* embodied in the principle of merit, (b) the *background fairness* embodied in the equal life chances principle, and (c) the claim of *liberty* defined by the autonomy of families principle. Each of the other process equalities mentioned is susceptible to a parallel construction. Each involves a *formal competition* for the consideration of claims in which an attempt is made to insulate the decision-making process from irrelevant factors. Just as the principle of merit defines one such formal competition, formal political equality, equality before the law, and the equal allocation of services and benefits in a nationalized health care system can all be construed in terms of such formal competitions—designed to institutionalize equal consideration for everyone's relevant claims. In each case, then, there is a recognizable issue of procedural fairness.

Once a formal competition is institutionalized in a context of social and economic inequalities, however, an issue of the second kind, of background fairness, also arises. The general point is that persons from the higher strata may have unequal

opportunities to acquire the characteristics or gather the resources and assistance that make for success in the formal
competition. When persons from the higher strata achieve this
kind of disproportionate success, the second element, the issue
of background fairness, arises.

The third element, liberty, comes into play, because disproportionate success in the formal competition (defined, for
example, by merit, political equality, or equality before the
law) could be prevented by the restriction of certain liberties.
In the political sphere these liberties include free speech and
association, and in the legal and medical care spheres they
include the liberties presently defining lawyer-client and doc-
tor-patient relations. These liberties parallel the liberties at
issue with the family for the equal opportunity case because
they affect the informal acquisition of characteristics or resources that claimants are able to bring to bear upon the more
formal process. Given social and economic inequalities, the
general problem is that procedural and background fairness in
these process equalities can only *both* be maintained at a cost
in liberty. How the sacrifice in liberty compares to the value of
fully implementing each of these process equalities remains an
open question that must be faced for each process equality in
turn. I have focused on the equal opportunity case, in part,
because the liberty in question is a central one whose implications for ideal theory have not been explicitly faced. If some of
the other liberties at stake in parallel cases are less important,
then those particular process equalities could be fully realized
at a less substantial cost in liberty.

Nearly an entire book was needed to sort through the complexities in this trilemma in a single issue area, equal opportunity. In this concluding chapter, I can only suggest how parallel
cases might apply to other issue areas. Let us pursue this
comparison in more detail for the central liberal principle of
political equality.

A variety of electoral systems can be devised that give each
citizen's vote equal weight in a formal sense. Proportional
representation offers one ideal. One-man, one-vote, in equal

population districts offers another familiar if less demanding ideal—subscribed to for the House, but not for the Senate, in this country.[13] Yet no matter how perfect the degree of formal equality, as this might be ascertained from the structure of the electoral system without any reference to the way persons with differing preferences are distributed within it, effective political equality requires something more.

It requires some effort to equalize capacities or opportunities to influence the informal processes that determine the substance of politics—the taking of positions, the setting of agendas, the gathering of political resources, the formation of public opinion. All of these informal processes may be subject to systematic inequalities of influence even when the design of the electoral system is as close to formal political equality as might be imagined.[14]

Consider Lindblom's "circularity" thesis, that major corporations, and persons in the higher strata who share their interests, have a "disproportionate influence" on both decision-making processes and the formation of public opinion in American society. Most importantly with respect to public opinion, Lindblom raises

> the ominous specific possibility that popular control in both market and government is in any case circular. It may be that people are indoctrinated to demand—to buy and to vote for—nothing other than what a decision-making elite is already disposed to grant them. The volitions that are to guide leaders are formed by the same leaders.[15]

13. For a systematic review of criteria for formal political equality see Jonathan Still, "Political Equality and Election Systems," in Fishkin, ed., *Theory and Practice of Representation.*

14. Note that this formula does not commit itself to fully equalizing influence. A theory that prescribed equal *opportunities* for influence (regardless of irrelevant factors such as income or class) would be more defensible. See my objection below that "those with similar interests and competence who differ greatly in their resources will also differ greatly in their opportunities to influence each of these processes."

15. Lindblom, *Politics and Markets,* p. 202.

Needless to say, political equality in any meaningful sense would be undermined to the extent that such a "circularity" thesis applied. The degree of the problem in America is a continuing controversy.[16] Whatever its precise dimensions, few would deny that there are significant spill-over effects from socioeconomic inequalities onto each of the informal political processes we have' mentioned—the taking of positions, the setting of agendas, the gathering of political resources, and the formation of public opinion. What is disturbing in terms of political equality is that socioeconomic position in general, and money in particular, serve to *magnify* the influence of some persons on each of these informal processes. Citizens do not have equal opportunities to influence each of these processes because those with similar interests and competence, who differ greatly in their resources, will also differ greatly in their opportunities to influence each of these processes. Some speak with magnified voices because "money talks"—in campaign contributions to independent groups, independent expenditures, and ownership of, and influence on, the media.[17] This magnification has an influence not only on specific decisions but also upon the formation of public opinion, on the definition of ground rules for public debate, and on the kinds of questions and positions that can reasonably expect to get a hearing. All of these informal processes raise the issue of background fairness no matter how strictly formal political equality is maintained.

Of course one might attempt, as we have in some post-Watergate reforms establishing political contribution and expenditure limitations, to insulate some of these political processes from background inequalities.[18] Yet the Supreme Court,

16. For a shrill counterattack on Lindblom's thesis see Eugene Bardach, "Pluralism Revised," *Commentary* 66 (August 1978), pp. 68–70.

17. For a recent review of the role of money in these processes see Michael J. Malbin, ed., *Parties, Interest Groups and Campaign Finance Laws* (Washington, D.C.: American Enterprise Institute, 1980).

18. For a comprehensive assessment, see *An Analysis of the Impact of the Federal Election Campaign Act, 1972–78*, (Cambridge: The Institute of Politics, John F. Kennedy School of Government, Harvard University, 1979).

in *Buckley* v. *Valeo*, in upholding some and overturning some of these efforts, noted rightly that all of them required, in varying degrees, sacrifices in liberty. Sacrifices in both liberty of speech and association would be required by any thorough effort to insulate the political process from background inequalities.

Consider the connection between money and speech. As the Court emphasized:

> Virtually every means of communicating ideas in today's mass society requires the expenditure of money. The distribution of the humblest handbill or leaflet entails printing, paper and circulation costs. Speeches and rallies generally necessitate hiring a hall and publicizing the event. The electorate's increasing dependence on television, radio and other mass media for news and information has made these expensive modes of communication indispensable instruments of effective political speech.[19]

Because of the pervasive role of money, restrictions on contributions or expenditures would have the effect of restricting speech. As the Court noted with respect to expenditures:

> Being free to engage in unlimited political expression subject to a ceiling on expenditures is like being free to drive an automobile as far and as often as one desires on a single tank of gasoline.[20]

Even the contribution limitations which the Court upheld were considered an important sacrifice of liberty, one that the Court argued, however, was outweighed by other even more important factors.[21]

In addition to freedom of expression, freedom of association is also clearly at stake.

> Contribution and expenditure limitations also impinge on protected associational freedoms. Making a contribution,

19. 424 U.S. 1, 19 (1976).
20. Ibid., at 19, n. 18.
21. Ibid., at 24–29.

like joining a political party, serves to affiliate a person with a candidate. In addition, it enables like-minded persons to pool their resources in furtherance of common political goals.[22]

The McCarthy presidential campaign of 1968 was cited to show how the freedom of association involved in political contributions may be a significant one in that it serves to increase the *diversity* of candidates and causes in the political spectrum. As Heard notes more generally of campaign contributions, "the traditional fat cats are not all of one species, allied against common adversaries. Big givers show up importantly in both parties and on behalf of many opposing candidates."[23] Stewart Mott and Martin Peretz have been as prominent in their support of liberal causes as W. Clement Stone and Walter Annenberg have been in their support of more conservative ones. And large initial contributions may be crucial in launching campaigns that might otherwise die stillborn. Julian Bond's campaign manager was cited in the Buckley briefs because he blamed the new contribution restrictions for his inability to gather enough "seed money" for a presidential campaign.[24] And the same brief also employed the McCarthy example:

> The 1968 presidential campaign of appellant Eugene McCarthy is a paradigm case of why contributions to a candidate are protected by the First Amendment. Individuals who contributed to the McCarthy campaign in order to further the cause of terminating the war in Southeast Asia were able to pool their resources in the most effective way available at that time. If each had been required to act only as a volunteer, or to contribute only to "issue" organi-

22. Ibid., at 23.
23. Alexander Heard, *The Costs of Democracy* (Chapel Hill: University of North Carolina Press, 1960), p. 6; also cited in Appellant's Brief, Buckley v. Valeo, p. 62.
24. Appellant's Brief, Buckley v. Valeo, pp. 61–62.

zations not supporting a candidate . . . contributors as a result would have been far less able to further the cause in which they believed so strongly. Campaign contributions were thus a means of exercising the freedom of association as well as the freedom of expression.[25]

Despite these arguments, the Court upheld contribution limitations, believing that the cost in liberty was worth the other goals served (greater equality of influence, reduction in the incidence and appearance of corruption, and so forth).[26] Yet these examples show that the liberty to make political contributions that was thus restricted may also have an impact on the *variety* of causes and candidates supported in the political system. It is not only X's liberty to join in a cause with Y that may be restricted; the liberty of another who is unaffiliated, such as Z, to hear the political messages resulting from such a campaign (and perhaps to join) may also be affected.

Of course, any effort to insulate public opinion formation from background inequalities would also have to intrude upon contributions, expenditures, and acts of expression by other individuals than those directly involved in campaigns and on other issues than those directly relevant to particular campaigns. The Court struck down limits on independent expenditures as a violation of the First Amendment. And in *First National Bank* v. *Belotti*, the Court held that in "the realm of protected speech, the legislature is constitutionally disqualified from dictating the subjects about which persons may speak and the speakers who may address a public issue." Under this broad conception, the Court significantly extended First Amendment protections to corporations.[27]

Whether or not corporations (rather than individuals within them) should be given such First Amendment protection, it should be clear that any thorough attempt to insulate the

25. Ibid. at 49.
26. 424 US at 24–29.
27. 435 US (1978) at 784–85.

process of public opinion formation from economic inequalities would require a systematic sacrifice in liberties of speech and association applying to individuals. These liberties can be placed within the framework of the harm principle employed earlier. Persons or groups X and Y who wish to engage voluntarily in expression, to combine resources, or to form groups to promote causes should be free to do so, according to this notion of liberty, as long as they do not directly and significantly harm others. Now perhaps these liberties of expression and association need to be restricted or controlled in the interests of political equality but it is important to realize that the sacrifice in liberty is a real one. If the influence of economic inequalities on politicians—an influence that is indirect as well as direct—were ever to be eliminated, the required coercive restrictions on free expression and association would be quite enormous. Campaign contributions are only the most obvious and most direct influence. Even with strict public financing, one might imagine a Lindblomian process of circularity maintaining itself through unequal influences on opinion formation. But any more thorough effort to eliminate private money from political expression, broadly construed, would require a systematic sacrifice of first amendment freedoms of the sort that has never been seriously contemplated in this society. Such a thorough going effort would have to squarely face questions of media ownership, as well. As the appellant's brief in the *Buckley* case noted:

> It is totally irrational to permit William Loeb, publisher of the Manchester Union Leader, broad freedom to attack a candidate while restricting the right of that candidate's supporters to employ economic resources in defense. The concern of the court below that the "wealthy few" not have "a stronger political voice than the unwealthy many . . . " is a concern which strikes as directly at the press and electronic media as at campaign contributions.[28]

28. Appellant's Brief, Buckley v. Valeo, p. 126.

Even if campaign contributions and expenditures were strictly limited, and even if Political Action Committees and issue advertising were eliminated entirely, unequal influences resulting from media ownership would have to be confronted. In a technologically complex society, where significant speech is seldom defined as the isolated man on a soap box, but rather as the newspaper article or editorial, or the television program or advertisement, eliminating the spill-over effects of unequal resources onto the formation of public opinion would require a host of restrictions on liberty of expression and association. Far from advocating such systematic restrictions, I mean to show that the liberties at stake in this form of insulation are comparable in importance to the liberties at stake in the autonomy of the family. Realization of political equality in more than a formal sense, like realization of equal opportunity in more than a formal sense (as specified by the merit principle), would require systematic confrontation with the spill-over effects from background inequalities. These can only be controlled at some considerable cost in liberty, either from insulation or, as we saw earlier in section 4.4, from leveling so as to eliminate the background inequalities directly.

The same analogy can be developed with other process equalities such as equality of consideration before the law or from the health care system.[29] In each of these cases spill-over effects depend on the freedom of persons from the higher strata to freely contract for superior services with legal or health care professionals whose superior skills and resources are attracted by the resulting market incentives. While the Legal Services Corporation and Medicaid exemplify the recent progress we have made in leveling up efforts for the poor in both fields, by

29. For an interpretation of American constitutional theory in terms of the right to "treatment as an equal," see Ronald Dworkin, *Taking Rights Seriously* (Cambridge: Harvard University Press, 1977), especially chapter 12. For a Rawlsian approach to health care, see Norman Daniels, "Health Care Needs and Distributive Justice," *Philosophy and Public Affairs* 10, no. 2 (Spring 1981): 146–79.

any realistic appraisal, such efforts could never aspire to full equalization—unless they were accompanied by systematic restrictions on the freedom of the non-poor to contract for better services. Such restrictions have never been palatable; even the National Health Service in Britain has had to tolerate coexistence with a system of private clinics for those who wish to pay for them.

In each of these cases the basic liberal idea of equal consideration can only be imperfectly institutionalized for a given process equality because of spill-over effects from socioeconomic inequalities. Insulation from these background inequalities could only be accomplished through restrictions on liberty. We must either accept the costs in liberty or accept compromise in the procedural or background fairness embodied in the process equality. These are the three general options in the trilemma. The only remaining possibility is the alternative sacrifice in liberty (discussed in section 4.4) that would result from leveling, from eliminating background inequalities directly. This latter possibility only demonstrates the truly radical character of each of the core process equalities when taken seriously.

Could a defensible version of liberalism accept compromise of equal opportunity, political equality, or equality before the law as a matter of *ideal* theory? Even though one's initial reaction to such a question is likely to be negative, the sacrifice in liberty in at least some of these cases is equally daunting. The required restrictions on the family or on freedom of expression and association (for equal opportunity and political equality, respectively) look far from inspiring for any adequate embodiment of the liberal ideal.

To what extent should we expect a solution to these recurring conflicts between liberty and equality? If the notion of equality were equality of outcomes rather than merely the process-related equalities explored here, then the problem posed by our general trilemma would not be surprising. Libertarians have made the conflict between liberty and equality of

outcomes a commonplace of recent political theory. It is, I
believe, more surprising and disturbing that the apparently
more modest process equalities considered here, if taken seriously, pose conflicts with liberty that are equally stark and
unavoidable. Let us now turn to the kinds of solutions to these
recurring conflicts that might be expected from further efforts
to develop liberal political theory. In particular, let us examine
some recent attempts to perfect the liberal notion of a process
equality—the liberal notion of a procedure granting everyone's
claims equal consideration—in *hypothetical* versions designed
to choose first principles for organizing society. Perhaps these
hypothetical versions can surmount the difficulties of fully
institutionalizing such process equalities, given background
inequalities. However, while such hypothetical process equalities represent a valuable methodological strategy, I will argue
that they should not be counted on for any new and systematic
solution to the problems discussed here.

5.2 Living with   W hat kinds of solutions
Inconclusiveness   should we expect to these
recurring conflicts? This question takes us into a kind of issue
quite different from those we have focused on in most of this
essay. Thus far, we have concentrated on the *normative ethics*
of social choice—substantive questions of what policies ought
to be chosen by social institutions and political actors. We are
now entering a different area usually distinguished from normative ethics under the heading of *meta-ethics*.[30] What is the
basis for ethical judgments of a given kind and what are their
general defining features? These are meta-ethical questions
that can be discussed independently from the particular substantive content of the moral judgments under discussion.

30. The distinction between meta-ethics and normative ethics is a standard
one. See, for example, Richard B. Brandt, *Ethical Theory* (Englewood Cliffs,
N.J.: Prentice-Hall, 1959), pp. 4–10; and William K. Frankena, *Ethics*, 2nd ed.
(Englewood Cliffs, N.J.: Prentice-Hall, 1973), pp. 4–5.

In this concluding section of a work that is primarily normative rather than meta-ethical, I cannot deal systematically
with this vast subject. I believe, however, that I can briefly
introduce certain distinctions that will place the rest of the
discussion within a useful framework.

Let me distinguish three meta-ethical claims that are commonly made on behalf of moral or political principles.[31] I will
then argue that the possible consistent positions on these
claims reduce to four. The resultant scheme of four ethical (or
meta-ethical) positions provides a framework for evaluating
the kinds of answers we might expect to the conflicts explored
here.

The strongest claim commonly made on behalf of a moral
position is:

1. *The claim that one's principles are absolute, in other*
words, that their inviolable character is rationally un-
questionable.

By "inviolable" I mean principles that it would always be
wrong to violate.[32] One is never morally justified, in other
words, in overruling such absolute principles. In addition to
being inviolable, an absolute principle is also "rationally unquestionable." By this I mean that it is not open to reasonable
disagreement. Perhaps it is a necessary truth, if such a thing is
possible in ethical matters. Or if not a necessary truth, it has a
kind of apodeictic basis that renders further skepticism inap-

31. While this scheme will be applied to political principles, or ethical
criteria for social choice, it can be applied just as easily to moral principles for
individual choice.

32. Violating such a strong principle, even when it conflicts with another, is
morally prohibited. Conflicts among principles of this kind may, of course,
create blind-alley situations, where nothing one could do would be right or
morally acceptable. Such situations define a kind of tragedy. See Bernard
Williams, *Problems of the Self* (Cambridge: Cambridge University Press,
1973), especially pp. 172–74 for an account of cases of extreme moral conflict
in which the requirements of the overridden principles must still be faced in
some way. Even if one cannot follow a principle, because it conflicts with
another, one ought to make amends, experience regret, and so forth.

propriate. Of course, any particular position that laid claim to this characteristic would have to include a further account of the meaning of "rational" or "reasonable" and a further account of the basis for the principle's immunity from reasonable questioning. But these details of particular positions need not concern us at the moment.

A second, less demanding claim would weaken the absolutist character of the basis attributed to one's principles. I will identify it as:

2. *The claim that one's principles are inviolable, or that it would be objectively wrong ever to violate (permit exceptions to) them.*

According to the second claim, one may attribute an "objective" basis to principles that hold without exception. This objective basis, that we still need to clarify, however, falls short of the first absolutist claim of being rationally unquestionable.

A third, even less demanding claim may be identified as:

3. *The claim that one's principles are objectively valid, in other words, that they are supported by considerations that anyone should accept, were they to view the problem from what is contended to be the appropriate moral perspective.*

This claim no longer includes the inviolability requirement. Hence, such principles do not purport to be immune from justified exceptions or overriding. For example, in cases of conflict between principles of this kind, it may be right to override one principle for the sake of fulfilling another.[33]

---

33. Weak or prima facie principles may justifiably be overriden in cases of conflict. A conception of an action's being right "on balance" can be employed for such conflicts. One might still be required to make amends, to the extent possible, for the overriden principles, but principles of this kind would not define tragic or blind-alley situations (in which nothing one could do would be right).

But such principles, even though not inviolable, fall under a claim of objective validity (as do principles conforming to the second claim). The proponent of such a principle claims that from the appropriate moral perspective, one that he believes should have jurisdiction over anyone else's choice of principle (one that, in other words, he believes to be valid for anyone), there is sufficient support for the adoption of his principle.[34] This notion of the "appropriate moral perspective" may be formalized in a moral decision procedure such as Rawls's original position or the perfectly sympathetic spectator of the utilitarians. I shall explore such decision procedures below. Or it may be simply the informal appeal to impartiality familiar from the Golden Rule or from appeals that one should look at a situation from the perspective of the others affected. As Thomas Nagel characterizes it, "the general form of moral reasoning is to put yourself in other people's shoes."[35] However formal or informal such notions of the moral point of view, the idea of such an appropriate moral perspective provides the basis for a claim that a given principle has a kind of objective validity. Of course, proponents of different principles may have quite different notions of the appropriate moral perspective from which principles ought to be derived or chosen; but that is only another way of saying that the objective validity claim (3, above) is far weaker than the absolutist claim (1, above). It is weaker in that there is no claim that the basis for the principle is beyond reasonable question. Unlike the first position, no immunity from rational disagreement is claimed for the crucial assumptions, the "appropriate moral perspective" from which the principle can be supported.[36]

As defined, the properties mentioned in these claims stand in certain logical relations. An "absolute" principle must also

34. Even though particular accounts of the appropriate moral perspective may lead uniquely to some particular principle, the claim of any such principle is inconclusive because of the jurisdiction and foreseeability problems investigated below.

35. Thomas Nagel, *Mortal Questions* (Cambridge: Cambridge University Press, 1979), p. 126.

36. See the discussion of reflective equilibrium below.

be "inviolable" and "objectively valid." In other words, a principle satisfying claim 1 must also satisfy claims 2 and 3.
Similarly, a principle satisfying claim 2 must also satisfy claim
3. The idea is that a principle satisfying any of these claims
must also satisfy those *following* it, but not those preceding it.

On the other hand, if a principle fails to satisfy a given claim,
it must also fail to satisfy those that *precede* it, but not those
following it. If a principle is not objectively valid, then it
cannot be either inviolable or absolute in our sense. Or if it is
not inviolable, it cannot be absolute. Failure to satisfy claim 3
implies failure to satisfy claims 1 and 2. Failure to satisfy 2
implies failure to satisfy 1. In general, satisfaction of a claim
implies satisfaction of those following it and nonsatisfaction of
a claim implies nonsatisfaction of those preceding it.

Either of these logical patterns would reduce the consistent
possibilities for combining these claims to the four positions
depicted below:[37]

	I	II	III	IV
	Absolutism	Rigorism	Intuitionism	Subjectivism
1. Absolutist claim	+	−	−	−
2. Inviolability claim	+	+	−	−
3. Objective va- lidity claim	+	+	+	−

37. Consider the first of these logical patterns for consistent positions—that
conformity to a given claim requires conformity to those following it. Let us
number the three claims, C_1, C_2, C_3.
a. C_1 is either + or −. If C_1 is +, then by the hypothesized pattern, C_2 and C_3
must also be +. Hence, the pattern + + + (position I).
b. If, on the other hand, C_1 is −, then C_2 may be either + or −. If C_2 is +, then
by the hypothesized pattern, C_3 must also be +. Hence, the pattern − + +
(position II).
c. If, on the other hand, C_2 is −, then C_3 may be either + or −. If C_3 is +, then
the resultant pattern is − − + (position III).
d. If, on the other hand, C_3 is −, then the result is the pattern − − − (position
IV).

Accepting all three claims produces a position we can call "Absolutism" (position I)—an assertion of rationally unquestionable principles that hold without exceptions or overridings. Kant offers a good example of such a demanding position.[38] Rejecting claim 1 but accepting the remaining two produces a position I call "Rigorism" (position II) because of its claim to apply objective principles rigorously, or without any exceptions or overridings. Rawls in the modern era and Bentham in an earlier one offer good examples of such a position applying objective principles rigorously.[39] If we reject both

---

Of course, this scheme of four positions emphasizes certain distinctions to the exclusion of others. Consider, for example, a position laying claim to rationally unquestionable conclusions about prima facie principles. Such a position does not fall under either absolutism or rigorism because its principles are not inviolable. It would have to be classified at position III, intuitionism. While this would be appropriate in some ways, the position asserts more than the defining claims of position III. Instead of principles that are merely objectively valid, it asserts principles that are rationally unquestionable. In other words, while these classifications *exhaust* the consistent possible positions on the claims defined here, they also may *conflate* under one classification positions that we might wish to distinguish, at least for some purposes. These conflation problems do not affect the use I will put the scheme to here.

38. Our "synthetic *a priori*" knowledge of morality is "categorical"; it is "unconditioned" and "apodeictic." Its principles hold "let the consequences be what they may." See Immanuel Kant, *Groundwork of the Metaphysic of Morals*, trans. H. J. Paton (New York: Harper and Row, 1964), pp. 79–84. As he explains the exceptionless character of a priori moral judgments elsewhere, they hold "with strict universality, that is, in such a manner that no exception is allowed as possible," *Critique of Pure Reason*, trans. Norman Kemp Smith (London: Macmillan, 1929), p. 44.

39. I take the term "rigorism" from Marcus Singer who means by it "that certain moral values hold absolutely or in all circumstances." Marcus George Singer, *Generalization in Ethics: An Essay on the Logic of Ethics* (New York: Atheneum, 1971), p. 228. As for the classification of Rawls and Bentham at this position, see Rawls, *Theory of Justice*, pp. 21 and 51 for his rejection of an absolutist basis. For his aspiration to satisfy the inviolability claim see his discussion of the priority problem in section 8. Jeremy Bentham's utilitarianism displays comparable single mindedness; see his *An Introduction to the Principles of Morals and Legislation*, (Oxford: Clarendon Press, 1907; first published 1789). For a new interpretation claiming that Bentham embraced different standards for social and individual choice, see David Lyons, *In the Interests of the Governed: A Study in Bentham's Philosophy of Utility and Law* (Oxford: Clarendon Press, 1973). Classifying him at position II for social choice, will be sufficient for my purposes.

claims 1 and 2 but accept claim 3 we find ourselves with one of the positions Rawls is most concerned to argue against, "Intuitionism" (position III). Lacking a single inviolable principle (or group of inviolable principles in lexical order), one may, nevertheless, lay claim to objective principles that are weak or prima facie, that is, principles that are capable of being overridden or traded-off, one for another. This position is often called Intuitionism because it requires a careful weighing of moral factors in each particular case.[40] Isaiah Berlin's advocacy of a "plurality" of irreconcilably conflicting ultimate principles offers a good recent example of this position.[41] Lastly, if we reject all three claims, we find ourselves in the category of "subjectivism" (position IV). The subjectivist does not assert objective principles in any sense. He makes no claim that his principles are supportable from some appropriately impartial moral perspective. Typically, he views his principles, if he has any, as arbitrary personal tastes or private whims that are not susceptible to justification. Since I have defined this category as a residual one, I might have defined further subdivisions within it.[42] However, these will not be necessary for our purposes here. Edward Westermarck in his *Ethical Relativity* and Sartre in his early existentialist period offer good examples of this position.[43]

40. See Rawls, *Theory of Justice*, pp. 34-40.

41. Berlin, *Four Essays*, pp. 167–72. This pluralism is really at the center of Berlin's political theory. See Bernard Williams's "Introduction" to Isaiah Berlin, *Concepts and Categories* (London: The Hogarth Press, 1978).

42. Subjective universalists might be distinguished from relativists who judge others according to values that *they* accept (or that the relevant groups accept). The amoralist who refrains from all moral judgments defines another subdivision. Since subjectivism (position IV) was defined by the rejection of all three claims, any of these positions would be compatible with the classification defined this broadly.

43. See Edward Westermarck, *Ethical Relativity* (1932; reprint ed., Westport, Conn.: Greenwood Press, 1970) Sartre's subjectivism is clearly expressed in "Existentialism is a Humanism," in Walter Kaufman, ed., *Existentialism: From Dostoevsky to Sartre* (New York: Meridan, 1956). A more recent argument for one variant of subjectivism can be found in Gilbert Harman, "Moral Relativism Defended," *The Philosophical Review* 74 (1975) and *The Nature of Morality* (New York Oxford University Press, 1977).

What are the methodological resources within liberal theory that might provide a solution in any of these senses (short of position IV) to the moral conflicts explored here? A direct appeal to intuition or conscientious moral opinion cannot be expected to resolve the conflicts in the trilemma of equal opportunity, or, indeed, those in the more general trilemma applying to other process equalities. The ingredients for these trilemmas all have a prominent place in common moral opinion and in public ideology. A direct appeal to those opinions provided the basis for my analysis. Some other methodological strategy would be required to resolve or overcome the normative conflicts revealed here.

In an earlier era, there may have been sufficient consensus on ultimate religious and metaphysical matters to support an absolutist public ideology. For example, the appeals to "self-evident truths" in the Declaration of Independence were not merely a rhetorical flourish; they depended crucially on religious assumptions ("Men are endowed by their creator . . ."). Morton White explains Jefferson's conception of "moral laws of nature":

> They were thought to be decreed by God; they were regarded as precepts for the direction of the voluntary acts of reasonable agents; and some of them were thought to be discoverable by intuitive reason.[44]

Hamilton was even more explicit. He described natural rights as "written, as with a sun beam . . . by the hand of the divinity itself; and [they] can never be erased or obscured by mortal power."[45]

But the operation of religious and ethical diversity in a pluralistic and liberal society has long since undermined the religious and metaphysical consensus required to support such

44. Morton White, *The Philosophy of the American Revolution* (New York: Oxford, 1978), p. 157.
45. Ibid., p. 80.

eighteenth century appeals to absolutism. Hence that consensus is no longer available as an unquestionable moral basis for a public ideology. It is also arguable that a truly liberal political theory could never rest upon such an explicitly religious foundation because some degree of neutrality by the state between such doctrines would be necessary for freedom of religion, presumably an important component in any recognizably liberal theory.[46]

At any rate, the direct appeal to conscientious moral opinion cannot be expected now to resolve our trilemma. Let us turn to the distinctive methodological innovation of recent liberal theory—the development of moral decision procedures for the choice of political principles. Such decision procedures can be viewed as a further development of process equalities that embody equal concern and respect, but in a perfected, *hypothetical* form in which all possible biasing contingencies are eliminated. Instead of merely focusing on the institutionalization of actual practices conforming to this idea of equal concern and respect in particular areas of life, the new strategy in recent liberal theory has been to construct a hypothetical arena of decision embodying the moral point of view where everyone's claims can be more perfectly adjudicated and where a uniquely adequate solution to problems of distributive justice can be reached.

This notion of a hypothetical decision procedure is what unites Rawls's theory of justice with modern utilitarianism, as developed by such theorists as Harsanyi and Singer,[47] and with

46. For a limited account of neutrality with respect to religion, see Philip B. Kurland, *Religion and the Law: Of Church and State and the Supreme Court* (Chicago: Aldine, 1961). For a more ambitious account of neutrality with respect to all theories of the good, including religion, see Ackerman, *Social Justice in the Liberal State.* For a critique of Ackerman's central argument, see my forthcoming article, "Can there be a Neutral Theory of Justice?" *Ethics.*

47. See John C. Harsanyi, *Essays on Ethics, Social Behavior and Scientific Explanation* (Dordrecht, Holland: D. Reidel, 1976), part A; and Peter Singer, *Practical Ethics* (New York: Cambridge University Press, 1979), especially chapter 2.

a modern utopian-egalitarian such as Bruce Ackerman (in his innovative book *Social Justice in the Liberal State*).[48] The general strategy can be identified as the construction of a hypothetical arena of decision for the choice of principles of distributive justice according to an impartial consideration of everyone's interests. This strategy offers the possibility of systematic theory that might move beyond the analysis of intuitions or commonly shared assumptions. Should we expect the development of these hypothetical decision procedures to produce a breakthrough resolving the conflicts in our trilemma? Can they be expected to *settle* the problem of distributive justice, at least within the confines of ideal theory?

However productive such decision procedures may be for some purposes, there are some fundamental reasons to expect their results to be inconclusive. We should not expect position I resolutions from them. But this should not be a cause for despair if the range of alternatives has been correctly identified here. Lacking position I solutions, we can aspire to the more limited claims of positions II and III without being forced into the arbitrary Subjectivism of position IV. I will focus on two sources of inconclusiveness that can be labeled the *jurisdiction problem* and the *foreseeability problem*. Afterward, I will return to the scheme of ethical positions just outlined.

The jurisdiction problem becomes apparent from the question: why should our ethical disputes be resolved by one particular hypothetical arena of decision rather than comparable others that can also claim to consider everyone's interests impartially?

Consider some of the possibilities. Rawls proposes an "original position" from which each of us can imagine ourselves choosing principles of justice out of rational self-interest while knowing nothing in particular about ourselves or about our place in society. A "veil of ignorance" shields each of us from

---

48. Ackerman, *Social Justice in the Liberal State* (New Haven: Yale University Press, 1980). See the discussion of neutrality below.

the knowledge that might permit us to bias the construction of principles toward our own particular self-interest. Rawls believes that this construction of the fair hypothetical choice situation, when combined with certain other assumptions, provides an argument for his particular proposed principles of justice. I won't enter the controversy here as to whether or not these assumptions actually yield Rawls's proposed principles.[49] I will only note that Rawls's argument, like other moral decision procedures in liberal theory, depends on both (i) a particular interpretation of impartiality (the veil of ignorance and other related conditions of the original position), and (ii) a particular interpretation of everyone's interests (Rawls's theory of "primary goods" that, he contends, it is in the interests of everyone to want regardless of whatever else they want).

The important point is that even if one were committed to the basic strategy of choosing principles of justice from a hypothetical arena designed to perfectly consider everyone's interests impartially, one would have to resolve the problem of why one particular interpretation of impartiality rather than another, and why one particular interpretation of interests rather than another, should be adopted for the design of the hypothetical decision procedure. Consider a slight variation. Rawls admits that a minor adjustment in his own proposed original position—an adjustment permitting probabilistic calculations—would yield the rival principle he is most determined to argue against, the principle of average utility. If one is permitted to assume that one has an equal chance of turning out to be anyone, then one's expected value of payoffs in life would be maximized by a society maximizing average utility.[50] This can be considered a modification in the interpretation of

49. See my "Justice and Rationality" for an extended discussion of this issue. In Rawls's most recent work, there is an acknowledgment of the morally controversial character of the argument from the original position in the claim that it depends upon a particular "model conception of a moral person." See John Rawls, "Kantian Constructivism in Moral Theory: The Dewey Lectures 1980," *The Journal of Philosophy* 77 no. 9 (September 1980): 515–72.

50. Rawls, *Theory of Justice*, p. 165.

impartiality (interpreted now so as to require an equal probability of being anyone) and a modification in the interpretation
of interests (interpreted now to mean satisfaction of preferences). Whether equal probabilities rather than mere uncer-
tainty (as in Rawls's proposal) is the more appropriate interpretation of impartiality or whether utility rather than primary
goods is the more appropriate interpretation of interests, are
not issues that can be decided by the decision procedure itself.
Rather, construction of the decision procedure requires some
independent basis for these decisions.

Ackerman provides us with still another interpretation of
impartiality and still another interpretation of interests. His
hypothetical choice situation is a dialogue for occupants of a
spaceship about to start life anew on an uninhabited planet.
They must determine the appropriate distribution of "manna,"
a substance that is "infinitely divisible and malleable, capable
of transformation into any physical object a person may desire."[51] But the crucial point about Ackerman's mental experiment is that the occupants must justify a particular distribution of manna by providing an argument that passes certain
constraints, the key one being an account of moral impartiality
that Ackerman dubs "neutrality," as follows:

> *Neutrality.* No reason is a good reason if it requires the
> power holder to assert:
> (a) that his conception of the good is better than that
>   asserted by any of his fellow citizens, or
> (b) that regardless of his conception of the good, he is
>   intrinsically superior to one or more of his fellow
>   citizens.[52]

Participants in this hypothetical dialogue soon discover that
the only argument that passes this neutrality constraint can be
summed up as "I'm at least as good as you are, therefore I

51. Ackerman, *Social Justice*, p. 31.
52. Ibid., p. 11.

should get at least as much."[53] And this argument is employed to justify equal shares of manna on arrival at the planet. Then, in a more complex consideration of the distribution problem over time, in real societies lacking the imaginary substance manna, Ackerman discusses "second" and "third best" approximations to the hypothetical ideal of the spaceship dialogue. In this way he is led to prescriptions for education, genetics, and initial material endowments that are analogous to the equal manna solution. The results are ingenious in their maintenance of diversity amidst a basic framework of strict initial equality. While the argument, like Rawls's, has proven controversial, the central point is that when a quite different but appealing conception of impartiality (neutrality) is combined with a quite different but appealing conception of individual interests (receiving as much manna as possible), a radically different principle of justice emerges.

A fourth hypothetical decision procedure offering a familiar account of how everyone's interests might be considered equally is the perfectly sympathetic and impartial "spectator" of the classical utilitarians. Going back to Adam Smith, this idea would have us imagine a spectator who reproduced in himself every pain and every pleasure in the world. Perfectly reproducing in himself every sensation of disutility and of utility experienced by anyone, he would prefer those states of the world that maximized the over-all balance of pleasure over pain. In this procedure, another account of impartiality (perfectly sympathizing with everyone's pain and pleasure in the same way) is combined with an account of everyone's interests (utility) so as to yield the familiar principle of aggregate utility.[54]

---

53. Ibid., section 14.
54. Rawls, *Theory of Justice*, pp. 183–92. See also Adam Smith, *The Theory of Moral Sentiments* (Indianapolis: Liberty Classics, 1969), pp. 22, 31, 33, 35, 36, 38, 41, 71, 161–62, 211, 228, 247–49, 352, 371, 422; and Roderick Firth, "Ethical Absolutism and the Ideal Observer," *Philosophy and Phenomenological Research* 12, no. 3 (March 1952): 317–45.

These are not, of course, the only attempts to construct moral decision procedures that might plausibly claim to consider everyone's interests impartially. Elsewhere, I have argued that procedures for cutting a cake fairly provide an analogy that can be developed into a moral decision procedure for distributive justice in a society. The intuitive idea is that just as the cake-cutter ought to determine the slices without knowing which piece will be left for him (after the others are permitted to choose theirs), a person might be imagined to determine social allocations without knowing which ones will be left for him after the others choose theirs. While this procedure would yield maximin (the principle that the minimum share should be maximized) under certain assumptions about the "cake," under other plausible assumptions about the interests at stake it can be interpreted to yield its own distinctive principle.[55]

Here are five distinct moral decision procedures: Rawls's original position, the average utility version of the original position, Ackerman's theory of neutral dialogue, the perfectly sympathetic spectator of the classical utilitarians, and my adaptation of the cake-cutter's procedure. Each of them embodies a distinct interpretation of what it might mean to consider everyone's interests equally or impartially; each of them rests on a distinctive interpretation of the interests to be assessed. Even slight modifications in either of these basic components can produce extraordinary differences in the resulting principle—as the debate between Rawls and the proponents of average utility attests.

Of course, these five procedures do not begin to exhaust the field. There is no limit in principle to the proposals that might be developed. And there are certainly other interesting ones that have been proposed.[56] Not knowing how many appealing

55. See my *Tyranny and Legitimacy*, chapter 12.
56. See Douglas Rae's "Court of Allocation" in "Maximin Justice and an Alternative Principle of General Advantage," *American Political Science Review*, 69, no. 2 (June 1975): 630–47. See also Thomas Nagel, *The Possibility of Altruism* (Oxford: Oxford University Press, 1970), p. 141 for a proposal in which the chooser is to imagine himself living all the lives affected, seriatim.

accounts of impartiality might be presented, nor how they relate to the many controversial conceptions of individual interests (see section 2.1 above), we are forced to compare decision procedures informally. Even if we were absolutely sure of our judgment about each procedure in turn, we could never know whether, after committing ourselves to a particular procedure and its resulting principle, some better procedure with different results might not be devised. I will return to this issue below when I discuss the foreseeability problem.

The jurisdiction problem yields inconclusiveness in the following way. Any proponent of any of the five principles just mentioned, or any proponent of any other principle who bases his argument on this kind of decision procedure, is open to challenge at the point of commitment to his proposed account of impartiality and of his proposed account of interests. Those who would champion different principles can always challenge whether a given procedure should have jurisdiction or whether another is more appropriate. And because each procedure can be connected to a different substantive principle (about which proponents in an ethical dispute will have differing convictions), adoption of one particular procedure can always be challenged on the ground that it is *biased* toward X's convictions rather than Y's. The result is always open to reasonable disagreement because good faith disputes over substantive principles can always find their parallel in good faith disputes over moral decision procedures, in other words, over the appropriate reasonable basis for resolving disputes. The issue of which procedure to adopt cannot be settled by the procedure itself. And given the variety of procedures, each one supporting a different substantive outcome, the mere invocation of a moral decision procedure supporting one particular proposal is not enough to settle a moral disagreement.

Yet another proposal is developed by Lawrence Kohlberg in his "Justice as Reversibility" in Laslett and Fishkin, eds., *Philosophy, Politics and Society, Fifth Series.*

Just as different arbitration panels can be expected to produce different results in, say, a labor management dispute, different moral decision procedures clearly yield different principles of justice. But in a labor management dispute, the jurisdiction problem can be solved either by mutual consent of the parties involved or by recourse to the mutually acknowledged authority of a court order. But for our moral decision procedures there is no basis for actual consent, and no mutually acknowledged source of authority, tying us to one particular moral decision procedure rather than another. There are only further moral arguments about what we ought to agree to, or about what our actual notions of morality would commit us to, if we thought about them as the theorist advocates.

Since Rawls has addressed this issue more explicitly than the others, I will pause for a moment to consider his response. There is a revealing ambiguity in his account of why we should accept his particular conditions proposed in the original position. In the last paragraph in the book, he says that "we do in fact accept" the conditions, or that if we do not, these are conditions that we still "can be persuaded to" accept:

> Finally, we may remind ourselves that the hypothetical nature of the original position invites the question: why should we take any interest in it, moral or otherwise? Recall the answer: the conditions embodied in the description of this situation are ones that we do in fact accept. Or if we do not, then we can be persuaded to do so by philosophical considerations of the sort occasionally introduced.[57]

And if we are not or cannot actually be "persuaded," what is the basis for binding us to the results of the procedure? Rawls has an easy answer for the "egoist" who does not commit himself to the procedure since we knew all along that egoism "is incompatible with what we intuitively regard as the moral

57. Rawls, *Theory of Justice*, p. 587.

point of view."[58] But if we do not accept the procedure because we would rather accept some *alternative* account of the moral point of view, some alternative decision procedure that offers what we regard as a more appealing account of impartiality or a more plausible conception of interests, then we have a jurisdictional challenge that cannot be handled as easily. At this point, Rawls can only invoke the claim of "reflective equilibrium," a claim that only postpones the issue another step.

"In searching for the most favored description of this situation [the decision procedure], we work from both ends," we are told. We are to construct the choice situation and carefully examine the results, adding one weak condition to another;

> But presumably there will be discrepancies. In this case we have a choice. We can either modify the account of the initial situation or we can revise our existing judgments, for even the judgments we take provisionally as fixed points are liable to revision. By going back and forth, sometimes altering the conditions of the contractual circumstances, at others withdrawing our judgments and conforming them to principle, I assume that eventually we shall find a description of the initial situation that both expresses reasonable conditions and yields principles which match our considered judgments duly pruned and adjusted. This state of affairs I refer to as reflective equilibrium.[59]

Yet if each of us conscientiously goes through this process and arrives at a different "reflective equilibrium," as presumably sincere proponents of the five moral decision procedures described above already have done, then reflective equilibrium becomes a framework for reasonable moral disagreement. It is a position with different substantive implications for different practitioners of the process. We have only to replace the

58. Ibid., p. 136.
59. Ibid., p. 20.

pronoun "we" with the pronoun "I" and envision the resulting dissension among conscientious proponents of these five procedures, and others that might be devised.

Of course, to claim that the development of such moral decision procedures leaves the result inconclusive—in the sense of leaving it open to reasonable disagreement—is not to claim that the result is entirely arbitrary. A contested reasonableness is quite different from an arbitrary whim. In other words, our principles can fail to fulfill the requirements for position I without providing any basis for concluding that they must, therefore, be subjective, in the sense of position IV. There are two remaining positions in between (positions II and III). Within this middle ground, a controversial family of reasonable solutions (whether inviolable or not) can be distinguished from the claim at position IV that every arbitrary taste must be as good as every other.

I will return to this issue below. First, however, I will turn to a related source of inconclusiveness, one that I have dubbed the foreseeability problem. For purposes of argument, let us make the heroic assumption that perfectly unbiased and competent moral judges are available who can correctly judge each particular moral situation presented them. We might imagine a panel of judges operating with perfect consensus; or perhaps we might imagine ourselves, endowed with such powers, as members of this idealized panel. They prescribe particular actions or courses of conduct from the alternatives available in each situation; they do not, however, go so far as to offer general principles that might prescribe solutions beyond each isolated case at hand. Even with this limitation it is an extremely optimistic assumption. My argument is that even were such perfect moral judges available to evaluate particular cases, we would still have to regard any general principles as inconclusive and open to being overridden or drastically revised.

This argument is designed to focus on the possibility of a method based on concrete intuitions or clear moral convic-

tions about particular cases. The jurisdiction problem discussed above challenges a contrasting strategy, that of positing
a *procedure* as the fundamental commitment and then deduc-
ing general principles directly from the procedure (or from the
procedure and the assumptions it permits, as in Ackerman's
dialogue). As we have seen, this strategy leaves the result open
to reasonable disagreement since the adoption of one set of
initial assumptions rather than another is open to contested
interpretations of the two crucial component notions of the
procedure—impartiality and interests.

Nevertheless, one might imagine a quite different strategy,
one based on generalization from particular cases, from particular intuitions, or conscientious moral judgments about what
ought to be done in specific situations. Just as the strategy of
positing a decision procedure and deriving its implications is
essentially *deductive*, the strategy of positing particular cases
and generalizing from them is essentially *inductive*. Rawls, as
we saw above, hopes that the two strategies will coincide in
reflective equilibrium. But a realistic appraisal of the varieties
of conscientious moral opinion and the varieties of decision
procedure apparatuses that might be devised to support them,
leads to the conclusion that reflective equilibriums are likely
to reflect a wide range of moral disagreements.

Furthermore, this inductive strategy faces a special limitation of its own. Any moral principle that might be generalized
from a finite list of particular cases must be vulnerable to being
overturned in the future, even if our judgments of particular
cases came from a panel of perfect moral judges. A general
moral principle, as opposed to a particular judgment (or a finite
list of particular judgments) must apply to an open-ended class
of possible cases.[60] Whatever descriptive dimensions are employed to identify alternatives favored by such a general principle, they must amount to an *incomplete description* of each

60. See R. M. Hare, *Freedom and Reason* (Oxford: Oxford University Press,
1963), chapter 3.

particular state of affairs or course of conduct prescribed. It is always possible that other aspects of the partially described states of affairs (or courses of conduct) will be of sufficient importance to override the principles. This vulnerability obtains even if the principle conforms perfectly to all particular decisions taken up to now by our hypothesized perfect moral judges.[61]

The difficulty can be dramatized with a story I will borrow from Lawrence Tribe. An English couple acquire a magic talisman, a monkey's paw, that will grant them three wishes:

> The couple first wish for £200; shortly thereafter a messenger arrives to inform them that their son has been killed in a factory accident and that his employer has offered £200 out of sympathy. Their second wish is that their son return; it is answered by a strange knocking at the door that the parents somehow know to be their son— but not in the flesh. The tale ends with the couple's third wish, that the ghost go away.[62]

The couple's three wishes, like the prescriptions in any principle of moral or political choice, pick out certain dimensions of the desired alternatives, dimensions that must incompletely describe the states of affairs obtaining when the desired choices are realized. Just as the couple had each of its wishes fulfilled but with accompanying factors so terrible that they were fulfilled to its extreme regret in those particular cases, so may any general principle be fulfilled but with accompanying

61. I have adapted the notion of a superhuman moral judge from Dworkin. Dworkin's "Hercules," however, has powers extending to the faultless construction of general principles. See Dworkin, *Taking Rights Seriously*, pp. 105–30. The argument also depends on familiar limitations of inductive inference made famous by Hume and Popper. See Karl Popper, *The Logic of Scientific Discovery* (London: Hutchinson, 1959), especially pp. 29, 369–70, and *Conjectures and Refutations* (London: Routledge and Kegan Paul, 1963), especially pp. 42–48.

62. Laurence H. Tribe, "Policy Science: Analysis or Ideology," *Philosophy and Public Affairs* 2, no. 1 (Fall 1972). The story appears on pp. 102–03 and Tribe employs it to show the limits of "literal-minded devices." He borrowed it from Norbert Wiener who used it to show the limits of technology.

factors so terrible that its proponents would view its fulfillment with extreme regret in particular cases.

In another work, I explored counterexamples that can be arrayed against most of the principles currently prominent in liberal theory—procedural principles such as majority rule and unanimity; structural principles such as equality, maximin justice, and utilitarianism; and absolute rights principles such as Nozick's side constraint theory. These counterexamples reflect the power of the monkey's paw in the parable just cited. They are each compatible with complete fulfillment of the states of affairs or courses of conduct specified by the principles under discussion. Yet in each case, *other* elements of the incompletely described situation or policy are so terrible that reasonable proponents of the principles under discussion would surely wish the prescribed result to be avoided in those cases.[63]

Of course, if we could somehow completely enumerate or foresee in advance *all* of the possible negative contingencies that might accompany the incompletely described states of affairs or policies prescribed by our general principles, then we could *reformulate* our principles to include exceptions or qualifications for those particular overriding contingencies. The difficulty is that we lack any theoretical basis for ever presuming that we have completely enumerated all the contingencies. Because any such identification must always be open to revision, any principles generalized from the particular cases already decided must always remain vulnerable to being overturned by the unforeseen overriding factors presented by some new case. Hence there is a crucial source of inconclusiveness applying to such inductive strategies just as there was a crucial source of inconclusiveness applying to the deductive strategies considered earlier.

It should be obvious that principles generated by either the deductive or inductive strategies just considered, like princi-

63. I have made this more general argument in *Tyranny and Legitimacy,* part 2.

ples generated by more direct appeals to intuition, will clearly fall short of the kind of conclusive solution required by position I. These strategies only provide a basis for inconclusive principles. Such principles, even if they are formulated to hold inviolably, must only lay claim to a tentative and controversial kind of validity—a kind compatible with positions II and III, but not with position I.[64] Such principles should either be subject to reformulation whenever contravening cases arise, or they should be formulated at the outset to hold only prima facie, to be traded off within a framework of conflicting principles.

Should this kind of inconclusiveness be a disappointment? There is a common tendency to believe that anything short of the absolutist position (I) must be entirely "relative" or "arbitrary," falling into some version of the subjectivist position (IV). The psychological literature on moral reasoning shows that this tendency is common among ordinary moral reasoners.[65] This tendency also reflects a long philosophical tradition. Kant, for example, believed that the only possible alternative to his absolutist account of the moral law was the acceptance that morality must be "merely a Chimerical Idea without truth."[66] And it has not been uncommon for more recent theorists to believe that the dichotomy between absolutism and subjectivism (sometimes also treated under the heading of relativism) must be exhaustive of the possibilities.[67] Leo

64. I assume that absolutist or rationally unquestionable principles presume to settle the questions to which they apply conclusively.

65. See Lawrence Kohlberg, "Continuities in Childhood and Adult Moral Development Revisited," in Paul B. Baltes and K. Warner Schaie, eds., *Life-Span Development Psychology* (New York: Academic Press, 1973), pp. 179–204; Elliot Turiel, "Conflict and Transition in Adolescent Moral Development," *Child Development* 45 (1974): 14–29; and my "Relativism, Liberalism and Moral Development," in Richard W. Wilson and Gordon J. Schochet, eds., *Moral Development and Politics* (New York: Praeger, 1980), pp. 85–106.

66. Kant, *Groundwork of the Metaphysic of Morals*, p. 112.

67. The overly simplified dichotomy between absolutism and relativism is criticised in Thomas London Thorson, *The Logic of Democracy* (New York: Holt, Rinehart and Winston, 1962), chapters 1–5, and in Shia Moser, *Absolut-*

Strauss offers an especially influential example. He attacked Isaiah Berlin's assertion of conflicting controversial principles as "a characteristic document in the crisis of liberalism—of a crisis due to the fact that liberalism has abandoned its absolutist basis and is trying to become entirely relativistic."[68] Strauss chided Berlin for straying into the "impossible middle ground between relativism and absolutism." Berlin would have been more honest, Strauss implied, if he had admitted that his rejection of absolutism committed him to nothing more than subjectivism or relativism.[69]

But if our principles fall short of absolutism, by itself, that fact is insufficient to trap us in subjectivism. Between the rejection of position I (absolutism) and the acceptance of position IV (subjectivism) there stand two other meta-ethical possibilities—positions within which all of us may struggle with our inconclusive and controversial convictions that are supportable from various objective perspectives. The possibility of reasonable disagreement requires that there be a role for reason, even if it is one that is insufficient to settle these questions in any conclusive way.

Unless the possibility of this middle ground is explicitly affirmed, liberal theory is rendered vulnerable to a kind of moral self-destruction—vulnerable to a delegitimation of itself as a moral ideology. The religious and metaphysical consensus that once might have supported an absolutist version of liber-

---

ism and Relativism in Ethics (Springfield, Ill.: Charles C. Thomas, 1968). Both offer exhaustive documentation of the prevalence of the distinction.

68. Leo Strauss, "Relativism," in Helmut Schoek and James W. Wiggins, eds., Relativism and the Study of Man (Princeton: D. Van Nostrand, 1961), p. 140.

69. Ibid. Strauss does not explicitly commit himself to the claim that the middle ground is "impossible." His position on the middle ground can be inferred, however, from the fact that Berlin is criticized for abandoning absolutism without thereby embracing relativism, and from the fact that the "crisis of liberalism" is diagnosed (in the passage cited) as "due to the fact that liberalism has abandoned its absolutist basis and is trying to become entirely relativistic" (emphasis added). The thrust of his position is that Berlin has not faced the relativistic implications of his rejection of absolutism.

alism has evaporated in the modern era. And the methodological resources available to contemporary liberal theory clearly fall short of any plausible absolutist claim. Hence, unless the middle ground positions between absolutism and sheer subjectivism are affirmed, a quite reasonable skepticism about position I would provide the basis for trapping us into position IV. The denial of conclusive principles would limit us to entirely arbitrary ones. Subjectivism denies *any* objective, impartial, or appropriate moral perspective from which our principles are rationally supportable. It reduces us to a position in which any moral perspective must be as good as any other, in which private preferences about justice or equality become indistinguishable in kind (although perhaps not in degree or intensity) from private preferences about flavors of ice cream.

A moral ideology that asserts such subjectivism must delegitimate itself by affirming the arbitrariness, the sheer subjectivity of its prescriptions. Modern and defensible versions of liberal ideology, by inevitably falling short of absolutism, will find themselves trapped in subjectivism—when they are also committed to, or when their proponents grant, *absolutist expectations* that require that something like position I be satisfied in order for what we have called position IV, subjectivism, to be avoided.

The affirmation and creative development of the middle ground, positions II and III in my scheme, are the best line of defense for liberal theory. Even if one were to arrive at no more of a solution to the substantive trilemmas than an acceptance of conflicting prima facie principles, to be traded off in particular cases, such acceptance would still provide the basis for a defensible liberalism. Once this interpretation of the metaethical alternatives is adopted, a possibility is granted within which liberalism can thrive as a defensible moral ideology.

In fact, without some further breakthrough, permitting a tentatively plausible rigorism (position II), we are left with no more than an intuitionism of conflicting principles, to be traded off in particular cases, a version of what I have been

calling position III. Admittedly, such a position is at an ideological disadvantage compared to many of its competitors. It
affirms a plurality of conflicting principles without adding up
to a single ideal or unified vision for the organization of
institutions in a just society. It lacks a unified program because
it lacks any general priority relations among its conflicting
parts. How its principles are to be balanced remains an open
question, to be faced in particular cases as they present themselves. It leaves unclear how much one conflicting principle is
to be emphasized, compared to another. It does not define a
general direction for public policy since it offers us no single
vision of social justice in clear focus. Rather than aspiring to
some new and systematic solution (some version, in other
words, of positions I or II), it embraces the conflicting principles in our trilemmas, to be balanced against each other in
particular cases.

Accepting such a plurality of values, to be weighed prima
facie against each other, even under the best conditions, would
represent a decisive lowering of expectations by the standards
of contemporary theory. Such a version of position III would
then be received by many as a disappointment or as a non-
theory;[70] for it fails to offer us a systematic solution, a vision of
the just society in clear focus to be gradually approached as
conditions permit.

This limited liberalism, offering us *ideals without an ideal,* a
plurality of principles without a unified vision, may be the
most honest response to the true difficulties of distributive
justice. A more rigorous and conclusive solution would only
glibly paper over dilemmas, or trilemmas, that will present
themselves in any case. It is in the spirit of an effort to clear
ground—where such an honest but limited liberalism may
thrive—that this book is offered.

---

70. As Rawls says "An intuitionist conception of justice is, one might say,
but half a conception." *Theory of Justice,* p. 41. For an overview of liberal
rejections of intuitionism see section 8 of that work.

INDEX

Absolute principles, 170–71, 172–75, 189

Absolutism, 174–75, 176–77, 178, 186, 190, 191–93

Ackerman, Bruce, 158, 178, 180–81, 182

Advantaged strata, 7, 55, 64, 66, 135, 159–60; and intervention strategies, 66, 68, 70, 71–72, 80, 82; and unequal talent development, 51–55, 61, 66. *See also* Minority groups

Affirmative action, 85, 95–96, 98. *See also* Compensation; Preferential treatment; Reverse discrimination

Aggregative principles, 15, 16, 122–23, 130; in group compensation, 124, 125

Annenberg, Walter, 164

Anti-Defamation League, 98–99

"Appropriate moral perspective," 172

Arbitrary native characteristics, 4, 5, 32–35, 87; defined, 28, 32; and preferential treatment, 93, 94, 95–96, 97, 105; and problem of assignment, 24, 25–30; as qualifications, 108–09

Assignment, problem of, 11, 13, 16–19, 45, 55–56, 67, 108–09, 132; equal opportunity and, 19–30; in lottery system, 59, 61–62; preferential treatment in, 85–87. *See also* Merit, principle of

Autonomy of the family, 5–6, 7–8, 33n27, 84, 89, 106–07, 108, 110, 132, 159; and background inequalities, 67–82; defined, 5, 35, 58; and development of talents and qualifi-

cations, 51–55, 62–63, 64–67; and equal life chances, 50–64, 104; and equal opportunity, 35–43; and liberty/equality conflict, 145–46; public policy re, 147–51; sacrifice of, in equal opportunity trilemma, 50–82

Background inequalities, 1–2, 3–4, 5, 6–9, 22, 84, 106–07, 129, 131, 157; cost to liberty in elimination of, 132, 144–46; and equal life chances option, 55, 61, 62, 64, 67; in political process, 162–63, 165, 167; and preferential treatment, 89–90, 93, 95–97, 105; process equalities and, 159–60, 167–68, 169; in trilemma of equal opportunity, 47–51; and unequal life chances, 51–55, 104. *See also* Arbitrary native characteristics; Preferential treatment

Bakke case, 21, 85, 87, 90, 95, 96, 97, 109n2, 149–50

Barry, Brian, 16n9, 22

Bentham, Jeremy, 174

Berlin, Isaiah, 39, 175, 191

Bickel, Alexander, 88

Blackmun, Harry, 147n51

Blacks, 18, 47, 86, 95, 148; and equal opportunity, 128–29, 152–53; as social group, 114–18, 122, 126

Bond, Julian, 164

Bronfenbrenner, Urie, 72–74, 75

Buckley v. *Valeo*, 8, 163–64, 166

Carens, Joseph, 137–43

"Circularity" thesis (Lindblom), 161–62

Coercive interference, 36, 38–42, 58,

Coercive interference (*continued*) 63, 64–65, 68, 79, 132, 166; and autonomy principle, 81; in freedom of property, contract, and employment, 140, 144; justification of, 39–40, 65–66, 77–78; in strict equality, 135; in preference formation, 141–42

Coleman, James, 68–69, 71

Compensation, 30, 46, 47, 67, 82, 96–105, 150; group, 113–31; intergenerational, 117–18

Competition, 107, 159–60; and lotteries, 110–13; and compensation, 113–31. *See also* Fair competition assumption

Consensual relations, 35, 36–38, 42, 43n45, 58, 135–36, 146; justification of interference in, 65–66; in marketplace, 139–40

DeFunis, Marco, 90, 98

DeFunis case, 21, 85, 87–89, 96, 149

Developmental conditions: differential, 51–54, 110; equalization of, 6, 32–33, 96–97, 152–57, 159; parental control of, 51–55, 62–63, 64–67; and preferential treatment, 89–90, 104–05. *See* Background inequalities; Qualifications, for positions

Disadvantaged strata, 8, 89–90, 92, 93, 94, 96, 99, 102–05, 119, 120, 121, 124, 149; moral claim of, 13n6, 14–16; social experimentation for, 147–49; and strategies of intervention, 67–68, 71–72, 73, 77, 105; targeting of benefits to, 149–50

Distribution of goods and welfare, 1, 122, 129–30

Distributive justice, 1, 2, 45–46, 133–35; choice of principles in, 177–82, 184, 193; three problems of, 11–19. *See also* Realistic budget constraint

Distributive principles, 12, 15–16, 19

Dorn, Edwin: *Rules and Racial Equality*, 128–29, 130

Dworkin, Ronald, 158

Edelman, Marian Wright, 88–89

Education, 40–42, 46, 68–75, 96, 148, 155; preceptoral, 140–41

Efficiency, 21, 137, 138, 144; and lottery system, 111, 112–13; and equality of life chances, 55–56, 61, 62–63

Egalitarianism, 3, 135, 137–39, 141, 144–45

Equal concern and respect for everyone, 158–60, 168, 169, 180–85; hypothetical versions of, 169, 177–82

Equal opportunity, 1–10, 146–47, 158, 168; autonomy of the family and, 35–43; blacks and, 128–30; cost to liberty of, 107, 132, 145–46, 160; defined, 128; equality of life chances and, 30–35; problem of assignment in, 19–30; radicalism of, 106–07, 146; Rawls's doctrine of, 154–58; strong doctrine of, 20–21, 145–46. *See also* Trilemma of equal opportunity

Equality, 13–14, 16, 17, 106–51, 158n12, 189; conflict with liberty, 2–4, 7–10, 132–46, 168–69; lack of, in modern society, 47–50; and the law, 6–8, 158, 159, 160, 167–68; leveling approach to, 14, 167, 168; and maximin, 157n11

Equality of life chances, 4–6, 7, 18–19, 20, 22, 30–35, 47, 84, 95, 106–07, 145; causal mechanism for unequal life chances, 53–54; and compensation for past discrimination, 96–97, 103, 104–05; defined, 32; and definition of qualifications, 108; and equalization of developmental conditions, 153, 154–57; fairness and, 107, 108, 109, 159; in group compensation, 120–21; and inequalities between groups, 128–31; lottery system and, 111–12; public policy re, 147–51; and sacrifice of family autonomy, 51–55, 64–67, 68; and sacrifice of merit principle, 55–64, 89, 108, 109

Equality of outcomes, 1, 3, 6, 48,

50–51, 106, 107, 168–69; cost to liberty in, 131–46
Ethical positions, 170–75, 190–93

Fair competition assumption, 1, 5–6, 19–20, 55–56, 84, 104–05, 153; fairness in, 22–23, 24–25, 26, 34; and group compensation, 113–14, 116–22, 125–31; and lottery system, 62, 110–13; and merit, 107–10; and preferential treatment, 89–90, 96, 114–15, 122–24, 127; public policy implications of, 146–51; and unequal positions, 131–46
Fairness, 5, 21, 34, 60; in assessment of qualifications, 28–30; background, 22, 107, 109–10, 152, 159–60, 162–63, 168; cost to, in equal life chances option, 55–56, 61, 62; and merit, 107–10; procedural, 4, 22–23, 24–25, 31, 85–86, 107, 108, 109–10, 111, 112, 159, 168. *See also* Equality of life chances; Merit, principle of
Family, the, 1–2, 3–4, 33, 35, 63, 75, 79, 168; defined, 36–37; and educational environment, 69–70; and equalization of developmental conditions, 51–55, 62–63, 64–67, 153, 154–57; equal opportunity and, 11–43. *See also* Advantaged strata; Autonomy of the family
First National Bank v. *Belotti*, 165
Fiss, Owen, 114–15, 116, 117, 120, 122, 123, 124, 127–28, 130
Foreseeability problem, 172n34, 178, 186–90
Freedom of property, contract, and employment, 63–67, 107, 111–13, 134, 135, 136, 138–40, 144, 145

Gill, Gerald, 148
Government and social institutions: intervention by, 3, 57–59, 66–82, 148–49; lack of ideal for, 193; moral demands on, 45–46. *See also* Coercive interference
Great Society program, 147, 152–53
Greenawalt, Kent, 91
Groups, 24, 30; competition among, and compensation, 113–31; genetic inequalities between, 33n27; proxy, for actual disadvantaged, 93–94. *See also* Minority groups

Haley, Alex: *Roots*, 100–02
Hamilton, Alexander, 176
Harm principle, 14–15, 39–42, 43n45, 140, 146, 166; in family intervention strategies, 37n32, 76–77; in government intervention, 36n28, 57–58; in sacrifice of merit principle, 135–37
Harsanyi, John C., 177
Hayek, F. A., 137
Health care needs: equal consideration of, 7–8, 45–46, 159, 160, 167–68
Heard, Alexander, 164
Herrnstein, R. J., 33n27
Houlgate, Laurence D., 37n32
Huxley, Aldous: *Brave New World*, 65

Ideal theory, 6, 8, 9, 30, 44–47, 53, 66, 178; compromise in, 150–51, 154, 160, 168–69; conflict of equal opportunity and liberty in, 146–47; departure from, in trilemma of equal opportunity, 82–84, 104–05, 106; lack of coherent, 10, 104, 106, 154, 193
Inconclusiveness, 10, 169–93
Indoctrination, 38n33, 45n1, 80–81, 141, 142, 143, 144, 161
Intimate relations, 42–43. *See also* Consensual relations
Intuitionism, 174–75, 176, 178, 186, 190, 191–93
Inviolable principles, 171, 173–75
Israel, 65n37, 124

Jefferson, Thomas, 176
Jencks, Christopher, 52–54
Jensen, Arthur R., 33n27

Jews, 98, 123–24
Johnson, Lyndon B., 152–54, 157
Jurisdiction problem, 172n34, 178–86
Justice, 20, 193; compensatory, 46, 47; intergenerational, 100–02, 117–18; retributive, 46; strict compliance, 44, 46–47, 52, 82, 147. *See also* Distributive justice; Maximin justice; "Patterned" principles

Kant, Immanuel, 174, 190
Kurland, Philip, 88

Legal Services Corporation, 94, 167
Leveling down strategies, 66, 67–68, 69–70, 71–72, 80, 82
Leveling up strategies, 66, 67–68, 78–80, 82, 154, 167–68
Liberalism (liberal theory), 1, 30, 43, 50–51, 84, 104, 168–69; conflict between liberty and equality at core of, 50–51, 132; in contemporary public policy and political theory, 152–69; departure(s) from, in response to trilemma of equal opportunity, 109, 110, 112–13, 133–34, 146–47; equality in, 2–4, 6–7, 8–10; limited version of, 9–10, 158, 191–93; negative liberty in, 39; options for, 152–93; problem of assignment in, 11, 19, 20; solutions to moral conflict in, 176–93
Libertarians, 3, 132, 137, 168–69
Liberty, 40, 50–51, 156, 157n11, 159–60; conflict with equality, 2–4, 7–10, 132–46, 168–69; conflict with, in lottery system, 63–64; cost to, in elimination of inequalities, 7–8, 9; cost to, in equality of outcomes, 131–46; cost to, in equal opportunity, 107, 132, 145–46, 160; cost to, in political equality, 163, 165, 166; cost to, in process equalities, 167–68; ethical positions re conflicts in, 170–75; negative, 39–40, 42, 43, 84, 135–37, 140, 146; private sphere of, 4, 39–40, 42–43, 47, 61, 62, 63, 65, 66, 107, 111, 145

Lindblom, Charles E.: "circularity" thesis, 161–62, 166
Lottery system, 57–58, 61–64, 110–13

McCarthy, Eugene, 164–65
Maximin justice, 13, 14–16, 17, 157n11, 182, 189
Merit, principle of, 4–6, 19–30, 51–52, 68, 84, 106–07, 132, 145, 159, 167; defined, 22, 107; and equality of life chances, 30–35, 55–64; and equalization of developmental conditions, 153, 154–57, 160; fairness and, 107–10; and family autonomy, 37; liberty of employment and, 112; and preferential treatment, 86–87; public policy re, 147–51; sacrifice of, 29–30, 89–90, 93, 94, 103, 104–05, 107–11, 114; sacrifice of liberty in, 136–37; and unequal life chances, 53–54
Meta-ethics, 169–70; and moral principles, 170–75, 192–93
Mill, John Stuart: *On Liberty*, 39–40
Minority groups, 85–86, 89, 113–14; advantaged, 92–93, 95–96, 97–98, 102, 122–23, 130–31; and preferential treatment, 90–95, 114–15, 122. *See also* Blacks; Preferential treatment
Mistargeting of benefits, 103–04, 105n93, 150; in group compensation, 121–22, 124, 130–31
Moderate scarcity, 44–45, 46, 47, 66, 82, 147
Moral conflict, 170n32, 171–72, 175, 176, 178, 183–86, 191
Moral decision procedures, 172, 174–75, 177–90
Moral principles: generalization of, 187–90; meta-ethical claims re, 170–75, 176, 191–93

Nagel, Thomas, 172
Neutrality (concept), 180–81, 182
Nonexistence, 41, 118–19. *See also* Persons, potential

Normative ethics (of social choice), 169, 170, 176
Nozick, Robert, 13, 125, 136n36, 137, 189; and strict equality, 133–36, 139–40

Objectively valid principles, 171–72, 173–75
Original position (Rawls), 59–60, 172, 178–80, 181, 182, 184–85

Parfit, Derek, 100n91
Paternalistic inferences, 12, 37n32, 65–67, 72
"Patterned" principles, 133–36
Persons, potential, 59–60; moral claims of, 100–02
Plato: *Republic*, 65
Political Action Committees, 167
Political equality, 6–8, 158, 160–67, 169
Political influence, 7–8, 159, 161–67
Political principles: meta-ethical claims re, 170–75, 176–77; moral decision procedures for choice of, 177–90
Positions, social, 12, 13, 16, 17–18, 19, 22–23, 55; ranking of, 32; and lottery system, 111–12; unequal, 1, 3, 104, 107, 109, 131–46. See also Fair competition assumption
Posner, Richard, 92
Powell, Lewis, 109n2
Preference formation, 139, 141–43
Preferential treatment, 21, 82–105, 108, 149; for the directly disadvantaged, 131, 149–50; in group competition, 113, 114–15, 120, 122–23, 127–28, 130–31. See also Affirmative action; Compensation; Disadvantaged strata; Reverse discrimination
Primary goods (theory), 11, 12n3, 28, 32, 179; income as, 143
Private-property-market (PPM) system, 137–38, 139, 140, 141, 143
Process equalities, 6–10, 158–60; conflict with liberty, 9, 167–69; hypo-

thetical versions of, 169, 177–82; radical character of, 168
Public policy, 9, 83, 106, 146–51; 153–54, 169, 193

Qualifications, for positions, 4, 5, 23–30, 52, 54, 62, 107–09, 112; defined, 108; development of, 3–4, 5, 20, 31–33, 61, 108, 150; equalization of development of, 6, 67–82, 96–97; and equal life chances, 34–35, 55–57; fair assessment of, 3, 23–30; and fair competition, 136–37. See also Developmental conditions

Race. See Arbitrary native characteristics; Blacks; Minority groups; Preferential treatment
Rae, Douglas, 16n10, 182n56
Rawls, John, 125, 143, 158, 174, 175, 177–78, 193n70; doctrine of fair equality of opportunity/family autonomy, 154–58; maximin justice, 13, 14–16; moderate scarcity, 44–45; original position, 59–60, 172, 178–80, 181, 182, 184–85; strict compliance theory, 46; strong doctrine of equal opportunity, 20, 21; theory of "primary goods," 11, 12n3, 28, 32
Realistic budget constraint, 45–46, 66, 68, 77, 78
Reflective equilibrium, 185–86, 187
Relativism, 175n42, 190, 191
Reverse discrimination, 55–56, 61, 85, 86–89, 92–94
Rigorism, 174–75, 178, 186, 190, 191–93

Sacrifice of principles: minimum condition for, 84–85, 89, 93, 94, 103–05, 149
Sandalow, Terence, 90, 91
Sartre, Jean-Paul, 175
Self-regarding sphere of action, 40–42
Separateness of persons, 2, 19, 107, 121–27, 131

Sindler, Allan P., 149
Singer, Marcus, 174n39
Singer, Peter, 177
Slavery, 60n34, 122
Smith, Adam, 181
Social duty, 44n1, 137–38, 139, 141–42, 143, 144
Social group, 120; blacks as, 114–18, 122, 126; preferential treatment for, 127–28, 130. *See also* Groups; Minority groups
Socialization, 138, 141–43, 144. *See also* Indoctrination
Solzhenitsyn, Aleksandr I., 126
Soviet Union, 59n30, 126
Sowell, Thomas, 93
Statistical discrimination, 24, 25
Strauss, Leo, 190–91
Structural principles, 11, 12–19, 189
Subjectivism, 174–75, 176, 178, 186, 190–93

Thoday, J. M., 33
Thought control, 141, 145. *See also* Indoctrination; Socialization
Tribe, Lawrence, 188
Trilemma of equal opportunity, 5–6, 7–10, 20, 33n27, 35, 44–105; in American public ideology and political theory, 152–58; basis of, 159–60; general version, 9–10, 176, 192, 193; options re, 51–67, 106–07, 154, 158; responses to, 106–51; strategies of intervention in, 67–105

University of California at Davis, 90, 94n85, 149–50
University of Washington, 87–89
Utilitarianism, 14–15, 16, 17, 121–22, 125, 172, 177–78, 189; aggregate principle, 13, 14–16, 17–18, 181; average principle, 60nn33, 34, 179, 182; sympathetic "spectator" in, 181, 182

Value, problem of, 11–12, 19, 32
Values, plurality of, 193
Voucher plan, 70–72

Walzer, Michael, 158
Westermarck, Edward: *Ethical Relativity*, 175
White, Morton, 176
Williams, Bernard, 30